SIMPLY SOUTHERN

FAMILIAR FOODS WITH A UNIQUE SOUTHERN FLAIR

✦✦✦✦✦✦✦✦✦✦✦✦✦✦✦✦✦✦ ❖ ✦✦✦✦✦✦✦✦✦✦✦✦✦✦✦✦✦

Copyright © 1998
Alagasco
2101 6th Avenue North
Birmingham, Alabama 35203
205-326-8187

Library of Congress Number: 98-093015
ISBN: 1-878561-27-8

Edited, Designed, and Manufactured by
Favorite Recipes® Press
an imprint of

FRP

P.O. Box 305142
Nashville, Tennessee 37230
1-800-358-0560

Book Design: Lynette Sesler
Cover Artist: Rachel Cowart Oliver
Project Manager: Judy Jackson
Art Director: Steve Newman
Project Production: Sara Anglin

Manufactured in the United States of America
First Printing: 1998 5,000 copies

CONTENTS

FOREWORD

MY FONDEST MEMORIES of growing up in the South are of being dressed up for church and the Sunday dinners after church. True Southern menus mostly consisted of fried chicken and catfish; turnip greens, mustard greens, or collard greens with pot "likker" (sometimes a mixture of all three greens); sweet potatoes; potato salad; hot "cat head" biscuits with milk gravy or Alaga syrup; corn bread, skillet bread, or hoecakes; caramel cake; pecan pie; banana pudding; and homemade ice cream. When everyone had finished eating, they would retire to the front porch to sit and converse with each other or the neighbors. Later, I would sneak around the back, come into the kitchen, and get another helping of banana pudding (I loved it then...and I love it now). Years later, my mother, affectionately known as "Mrs. Johnnie Mae," confessed to me that she knew all along what I was doing, but she just didn't let me know.

This cookbook, through the generosity of Alagasco, depicts the Southern tradition. Alagasco will donate the proceeds to local charities. My affiliation with Alagasco reminds me of the warm, comfortable feeling I would get while growing up with ten siblings and loving parents.

There was never a doubt that Alagasco would be named one of the 100 best companies to work for in America.

I don't cook with gas just because I love the company and what they have done for the community and for chefs in the South. I cook with gas because for over thirty-five years, I have found no better way of cooking.

Clayton Sherrod CEC, AAC

CHEF CLAYTON'S SIMPLY SOUTHERN MENU

She-Crab Soup (page 32)

Chicken with Corn Bread and Bourbon Pecan Stuffing (page 77)

Pickled Black-Eyed Peas with Peppers (page 120)

Kenya Greens (page 120)

Alabama Corn Muffins (page 51)

Peach Butter (page 56)

Sweet Potato Pie (page 142)

Iced tea with fresh mint

Café Brûlot (page 25)

4

PREFACE

• ❋ •

THE RECIPES FOUND in *Simply Southern* combine over ten years' worth of Alagasco's PIPELINE recipes, favorite dishes of many of our employees, more than ninety recipes for the grill, and a special Southern menu from Birmingham's well-known chef, Clayton Sherrod, CEC, AAC.

Our monthly bill insert, PIPELINE, has traditionally contained simple, easy-to-prepare recipes. Our readers have become so accustomed to these monthly recipes that we hear from them when we skip a month. Many recipes, such as our Corn Casserole on page 118, become family favorites. So for our loyal customers and everyone who likes to cook, we've compiled this collection of recipes for your enjoyment. And, since great menus are inspired by the foods we grew up with, we hope that some of these become traditions in your home.

Chef Clayton, owner and operator of Chef Clayton's Food Systems, Inc., has been affiliated with Alagasco for almost two decades. As executive chef, he has planned, organized, and catered all types of events, from small board of directors functions to large company picnics for more than 3,000 guests. Over the years, one thing has remained consistent: his commitment to serving the best food available. In 1997 Chef Clayton received the National Chef Professionalism Award, presented annually to the chef who exemplifies the highest standard of professionalism through certification, continuing education and training, culinary competition, and community involvement.

As our way of saying "thanks," proceeds from the sale of *Simply Southern* will be divided among local charities.

Connie Lyle Blalock
Manager of Graphics
Alagasco

 This symbol indicates recipes from Chef Clayton.

FACTS ABOUT YOUR GAS GRILL

GAS GRILLS make outdoor grilling easier, faster, and more energy efficient, to say nothing of fun and delicious. Current models have dual controls at fingertip level and automatic ignition. The backyard get-together with hot dogs and hamburgers can become a gourmet feast—with everything from stuffed mushrooms to angel food cake—all cooked on a gas grill, and...you can do it anytime of the year.

TIPS FOR GRILL USE

- There is no "one best way" to cook anything. Cover up? Cover down? Low flame? High flame? Experimenting is the key to success and pleasure in grill cooking.
- After a few cookouts, you'll learn the heat pattern of your particular grill. Use hottest areas for cooking, cooler areas for slower cooking and "keep warm."
- A moderate amount of flaring and smoking is desired to enhance barbecue flavor and appearance.
- Use your grill not only for grilling and as a rotisserie, but also for roasting, braising, frying, baking, and stewing—in foil, pans, and Dutch ovens (choose one with flameproof handles).
- Cook summertime meals on your gas grill to use energy wisely. An entire meal can be cooked at one time. Little or no cooking is necessary on your indoor range, so there is no additional load put on air conditioning equipment to cool down the kitchen.

Gas grills allow flexibility in cooking temperatures but will not provide the same exact temperature control as the oven on your gas range. Several factors can affect the heat pattern and speed of cooking on a gas grill:

- wind velocity and direction
- temperature of food at start of cooking
- outdoor air temperature
- location of grill
- preheat time
- cover open or closed
- size and shape of food
- preference for doneness
- distance between briquettes and food being cooked

DUAL CONTROL BURNER OF A GAS GRILL

The flame on each side of the dual burner is regulated by its own heat control. Follow the manufacturer's instructions for lighting. Usually, after one side is lit, turn on the other control to light that side.

The dual burner gas grill gives the option of cooking two ways, direct or indirect.

With direct heat cooking, the food is placed directly on the cooking grids. Steaks can be grilled on HIGH on one side while a casserole can be slow-cooked on the other side. Use only one side and save energy when preparing a small meal.

With indirect heat cooking, the food, in a pan or directly on the grill, does not come into direct contact with a flame. The cover is closed. Heat from the lighted side of the burner circulates gently throughout the grill, similar to the heat of your oven, and roasts or bakes the food. Advantages are that you don't have to worry about flare-ups and it's easy to collect drippings for gravy.

Some grills feature rotissing from behind the meat without flare-up. Direct heat reduces cooking time.

Grills can be purchased that feature carving stands, serving boards, condiment trays, slide-out utensil racks, ice chests, storage compartments, refreshment shelves, electronic timers, temperature gauges, heat-resistant handles, extra gas side burner, heavy-duty grill ovens, cookers, smokers, and clam bake models. Some grills offer a five-year warranty on specific features of the grill. Be sure to ask your dealer about these special features.

If your gas grill is not equipped with a dual control burner, you can enjoy this method of cooking by using heavy-duty foil to block off half the heat from the burner and briquettes. Take a sheet of heavy-duty foil twice as long as the cooking grid. Fold in half, then in half again. Firmly line half the cooking grid. This will effectively block the direct heat from that side of the burner. Place a cooling rack or a cookie sheet on the foil. Food can be placed directly on the rack.

This symbol indicates recipes tailored specifically for the gas grill.

7

ACKNOWLEDGEMENTS

We would like to extend special thanks to all these people for their contributions to *Simply Southern*.

Rose Anthony

Donna Britt

Clydene Dyer

Tammy Flowers

Marion Harder

Jessica B. Harris

Carolyn and James R. Hoppèr

Bonnie Lorino

Cherry Mathison

Gloria and Tony McLendon

Debra D. and Richard Minor

Renee M. Muhammad

Rachel C. Oliver

Janna Paslay

Janet F. Quick

Johnny Rivers

Debra Sloan

South Eastern Meats Inc.

Chef Frank Stitt

Willie M. Stubbs

Sherrie Tarpley

Diane Thomas

Jeanne A. Voltz, author of *Flavor of the South*

Anne M. Warren

Blane Weaver

Sharon J. Whittington

Gloria Woodard

Diane Youngblood

CHAPTER ONE

APPETIZERS AND BEVERAGES

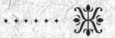

GRILLED APPETIZER LOAF

1 (8-ounce) loaf Italian or French bread
1 cup finely chopped ham
1/4 cup chopped stuffed olives
3/4 cup mayonnaise or mayonnaise-type salad dressing
2 teaspoons prepared mustard
pepper to taste

Cut a thin slice from the top of the bread. Hollow out the loaf, leaving a 1/2-inch shell. Tear the bread into small pieces into a large bowl. Combine the ham, olives, mayonnaise and mustard with the bread pieces and mix well. Season with pepper. Pack the mixture into the loaf; replace the top. Wrap the loaf tightly in heavy-duty foil. Grill on indirect heat for 30 minutes or until the filling is warm, turning occasionally. Cut into 1-inch slices to serve.

Yield: 12 to 15 servings

BITE-SIZE BUNDLES

8 pineapple chunks
8 dried apricot halves
4 dried figs, cut into halves
12 partially cooked slices bacon, cut into halves
1 1/2 cups orange juice or pineapple juice

Wrap each pineapple chunk, apricot half and fig half with 1 piece of bacon; secure with wooden picks. Place in a 9x13-inch baking pan. Bring the orange juice to a boil in a small saucepan. Pour over the fruit. Let stand for 30 minutes to plump the apricots and figs; drain well. Preheat gas grill using medium setting. Arrange the fruit in a hinged grill basket or thread on metal skewers. Grill for 10 to 15 minutes per side or until the bacon is crisp and cooked through.

Yield: 12 to 14 servings

CHEESE WAFERS

2$\frac{1}{2}$ cups flour
1 teaspoon salt
$\frac{1}{2}$ teaspoon red pepper flakes
1 cup butter or margarine, softened
1 pound New York sharp Cheddar cheese, shredded
$\frac{1}{2}$ cup finely chopped pecans

Sift the flour, salt and red pepper into a large bowl. Add the butter, cheese and pecans and knead well. Shape into 2 logs. Chill or freeze overnight. Preheat oven to 425 degrees. Cut the logs into thin slices. Place the slices on a nonstick baking sheet. Bake for 8 to 10 minutes or until crisp.

Yield: 50 servings

CHEESE STRAWS

1 (5-ounce) jar Old English sharp cheese
$\frac{1}{2}$ cup butter, softened
1 cup flour
$\frac{1}{2}$ teaspoon salt
$\frac{1}{4}$ to $\frac{1}{2}$ teaspoon red pepper flakes

Preheat oven to 350 degrees. Cream the cheese and butter in a mixer bowl until light and fluffy. Sift the flour, salt and red pepper together. Add to the cheese mixture and mix well. Spoon the mixture into a decorator tube fitted with a star tip. Pipe into strips on a nonstick baking sheet. Bake for 10 to 12 minutes or until lightly browned.

Yield: 50 servings

SKEWERED CHICKEN WITH PEANUT BUTTER DIP

1 clove of garlic, minced
2 tablespoons finely chopped onion
2 tablespoons soy sauce
2 tablespoons vegetable oil
1 tablespoon lemon juice
1/4 teaspoon ground coriander
1 boneless skinless chicken breast, cut into 1/2x5-inch strips
Peanut Butter Dip

Combine the garlic, onion, soy sauce, oil, lemon juice and coriander in a medium bowl and mix well. Add the chicken. Marinate in the refrigerator for 30 minutes. Drain well, reserving the marinade. Preheat gas grill using medium setting. Thread the chicken onto metal skewers. Grill for 10 to 15 minutes or until the chicken is cooked through, turning and brushing with the reserved marinade occasionally. Serve with Peanut Butter Dip.

Yield: 12 to 15 servings

PEANUT BUTTER DIP

1/2 cup creamy peanut butter
1/3 cup milk
2 tablespoons finely chopped onion
2 tablespoons flaked coconut
2 tablespoons soy sauce
1 tablespoon brown sugar
1/8 teaspoon hot pepper sauce, or to taste

Combine the peanut butter, milk, onion, coconut, soy sauce, brown sugar and hot pepper sauce in a food processor container or blender container. Process until smooth.

HAM APPETILLAS

16 ounces cream cheese
$1/3$ cup mayonnaise
2 tablespoons chopped green onions
2 tablespoons chopped green olives
1 package large flour tortillas, at room temperature
1 (2- to $2^1/2$-ounce) package sliced cooked ham

Mix the cream cheese, mayonnaise, green onions and olives in a bowl. Spread a thin layer of the mixture over each tortilla. Top each with ham. Roll up each tortilla tightly. Chill, wrapped individually in plastic wrap, for 3 hours to overnight. Cut into $3/4$-inch slices to serve.
  Yield: 30 servings

SAUSAGE PINWHEELS

1 (8-count) package refrigerator crescent rolls
8 ounces sausage
$1/4$ cup honey butter

Preheat oven to 375 degrees. Unroll the dough, leaving it in 4 rectangles; press the perforations to seal. Spread $1/4$ of the uncooked sausage on each rectangle. Roll each up as for a jelly roll. Chill until the dough is stiff. Cut each roll into 6 slices. Place on a greased baking sheet. Top each slice with $1/2$ teaspoon honey butter. Bake until golden brown. Serve warm.
  Yield: 12 servings

CRISP GERMAN MEATBALLS

1 cup mayonnaise
1/4 cup prepared mustard
8 ounces ground hot sausage
1/4 cup chopped onion
1 (16-ounce) can chopped sauerkraut, drained
2 tablespoons fine dry bread crumbs
3 ounces cream cheese, softened
2 tablespoons chopped fresh parsley
1 tablespoon prepared mustard
1/4 teaspoon garlic salt
1/8 teaspoon pepper
2 eggs
1/4 cup milk
1/2 cup flour
1 cup fine dry bread crumbs
vegetable oil

Mix the mayonnaise and 1/4 cup mustard in a small bowl. Chill, covered, until serving time.

Brown the sausage and onion in a large skillet, stirring until the sausage is crumbly; drain well. Press the sauerkraut between layers of paper towels to remove any remaining moisture. Combine the sausage mixture, sauerkraut and 2 tablespoons bread crumbs in a bowl and mix well.

Mix the cream cheese, parsley, 1 tablespoon mustard, garlic salt and pepper in a large bowl. Add the sausage mixture and mix well. Chill, covered, for 2 hours.

Mix the eggs and milk in a small bowl. Shape the sausage mixture into 3/4-inch balls. Roll the meatballs in flour. Dip each meatball into the egg mixture, then into 1 cup bread crumbs.

Heat 2 inches of oil to 375 degrees in a large skillet. Fry a few meatballs at a time in the hot oil for 2 minutes or until golden brown. Drain on paper towels. Serve with the reserved mustard mixture.

The meatballs may be frozen after being cooked. To reheat, arrange in a single layer on a baking sheet with sides. Bake at 375 degrees for 10 minutes or until heated through.

Yield: 30 servings

SAUSAGE BALLS

4 cups baking mix
1 pound sausage
4 cups shredded Cheddar cheese

Preheat oven to 350 degrees. Combine the baking mix, sausage and cheese in a large bowl and mix well. Shape into small balls. Place 1 inch apart on a nonstick baking sheet. Bake for 15 minutes or until the cheese bubbles and the sausage is browned and cooked through. Drain well before serving.

Yield: 10 to 12 servings

QUICK-AND-EASY QUESADILLAS

2 tablespoons olive oil
1 clove of garlic, minced
6 tortillas
$1\frac{1}{4}$ cups shredded Monterey Jack cheese
1 tomato, chopped
$\frac{1}{4}$ cup chopped green onions
$\frac{1}{4}$ cup chopped cilantro
$\frac{1}{4}$ cup chopped green bell pepper
1 cup salsa

Preheat gas grill using medium setting. Mix the olive oil and garlic in a small bowl. Brush on 1 side of each tortilla. Grill the tortillas on 1 side only for 3 to 5 minutes or until warm. Remove the tortillas from the grill. Top grilled side of each with cheese, tomato, green onions, cilantro and green pepper. Return to the grill. Grill until the cheese is melted. Cut into wedges and serve with the salsa.

Yield: 6 servings.

EDAM SHRIMP APPETIZERS

15 ounces Edam cheese
8 ounces shrimp, finely chopped
$1/4$ cup minced onion
2 tablespoons margarine
1 medium tomato, chopped
1 cup soft bread crumbs
$1/3$ cup raisins
2 tablespoons drained capers
$1/4$ teaspoon salt
$1/8$ teaspoon pepper
1 egg, beaten

Cut the cheese into $1/4$-inch slices. Chop and set aside $1/3$ of the slices. Line the bottom and side of a 1-quart round baking dish with the remaining cheese slices.

Sauté the shrimp and onion in the margarine in a skillet until the shrimp turn pink. Stir in $1/2$ cup of the reserved cheese. Add the tomato, bread crumbs, raisins, capers, salt, pepper and egg and mix well.

Preheat oven to 350 degrees. Spoon the shrimp mixture into the prepared baking dish. Sprinkle with the remaining cheese. Bake for 30 minutes.

Cool in the baking dish for 15 minutes. Invert onto a serving platter. Garnish with lemon slices and watercress. Cut into wedges to serve.

Yield: 30 servings

SHRIMP PROSCIUTTO

18 large shrimp, peeled, deveined
1 (9-ounce) package artichoke hearts, cooked, drained
18 slices prosciutto, cut lengthwise into halves
olive oil or vegetable oil
pepper to taste

Preheat gas grill using high setting. Wrap each shrimp and artichoke in a piece of prosciutto; thread onto metal skewers. Brush lightly with olive oil; season with pepper. Grill for 4 to 5 minutes per side or until the shrimp turn pink, basting with additional olive oil occasionally.

Yield: 12 to 18 servings

SASSY SNACKING MIX

4 cups bite-size wheat or oat cereal squares
2 cups small pretzels
2 cups shoestring potatoes
1 (3-ounce) can French-fried onions
3/4 cup grated Parmesan cheese
1 envelope ranch-style salad dressing mix
1/2 cup cold margarine or butter

Preheat gas grill using medium setting. Mix the cereal, pretzels, potatoes and onions in a 9x13-inch baking pan. Combine the cheese and salad dressing mix in a medium bowl. Cut in the margarine until crumbly. Sprinkle over the cereal mixture. Cover the pan with heavy-duty foil. Grill for 30 minutes or until the margarine melts, stirring occasionally to coat. Serve warm or cool.

Yield: 16 servings

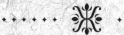

BACON-WRAPPED WATER CHESTNUTS

$1/4$ to $1/2$ cup soy sauce
sugar to taste
1 (8-ounce) can whole water chestnuts, drained
1 pound bacon

Mix the soy sauce and sugar in a shallow dish. Add the water chestnuts. Marinate, covered, in the refrigerator overnight. Drain well, discarding the marinade. Preheat oven to 375 degrees. Cut each bacon slice into halves. Wrap 1 piece of bacon around each water chestnut; secure with a wooden pick. Place in a shallow baking pan. Bake for 20 to 25 minutes or until the bacon is cooked through.

   Yield: 12 to 15 servings

ARTICHOKE DIP

1 (14-ounce) can artichoke hearts, drained
1 cup mayonnaise
1 cup grated Parmesan cheese
salt and pepper to taste

Preheat oven to 350 degrees. Break the artichoke hearts into pieces. Combine with the mayonnaise and cheese in a bowl and mix well. Season with salt and pepper. Spoon into a small baking dish. Bake until golden brown and bubbly.

   Yield: 20 to 25 servings

CHEESE ROLL

1 pound Velveeta cheese, cut into pieces, softened
3 ounces cream cheese, softened
2 tablespoons minced onion
1/2 cup chopped pecans
chili powder to taste
paprika to taste

Mix the Velveeta cheese, cream cheese, onion and pecans in a bowl. Shape into 1-inch rolls. Roll each in a mixture of equal parts chili powder and paprika. Serve with crackers.
   Yield: 20 to 30 servings

PIMENTO CHEESE

1 pound sharp Cheddar cheese, shredded
1 to 1 1/2 (2-ounce) jars pimento, drained
6 to 8 tablespoons mayonnaise
1/4 cup chopped onion
1/8 teaspoon garlic powder, or to taste

Combine the cheese, pimento, mayonnaise, onion and garlic powder in a food processor container. Process until creamy. Serve with favorite crackers or party bread.
   Yield: 20 to 30 servings

CHUTNEY CHICKEN SPREAD

1 envelope unflavored gelatin
$^1/_2$ cup milk
1 chicken bouillon cube
2 teaspoons curry powder
1 cup cream-style cottage cheese
3 ounces cream cheese, softened, cut into cubes
$^1/_2$ cup sour cream
1$^1/_2$ cups coarsely chopped cooked chicken breasts
1 (12-ounce) jar chutney
$^1/_4$ cup chopped celery
1 (2-ounce) jar chopped pimento, drained
$^1/_3$ cup chopped green onions
8 to 12 drops of Tabasco sauce
$^1/_2$ cup whipping cream

Sprinkle the gelatin over the milk in a small saucepan. Let stand for 5 minutes to soften. Add the bouillon cube. Bring to a boil, stirring to dissolve the gelatin and bouillon cube. Stir in the curry powder. Cool slightly.

Combine the cottage cheese, cream cheese and sour cream in a food processor container fitted with a metal blade. Process until smooth. Add the chicken, $^1/_2$ cup of the chutney, celery, pimento, green onions, Tabasco sauce and gelatin mixture. Process until coarsely chopped. Adjust the seasonings.

Beat the whipping cream in a mixer bowl until soft peaks form. Fold in the chicken mixture. Spoon into a 9-inch tart pan lined with plastic wrap. Chill until set.

Place the tart pan on a serving plate; remove the side of the pan. Process the remaining chutney in the food processor until nearly smooth. Spread over the chilled layer. Serve with crackers.

May be prepared in a 9-inch quiche pan if preferred.

Yield: 12 servings

HOT CLAM DIP

2 medium onions, chopped
3 (7-ounce) cans minced clams, drained
16 ounces cream cheese, softened
salt and pepper to taste

Process the onions with just enough water to mix in a blender. Pour into a nonstick skillet. Add the clams. Cook over low heat until the water is absorbed, stirring occasionally. Add the cream cheese, salt and pepper and mix well. Serve hot from a chafing dish with crackers or corn chips.

Yield: 20 servings

CRAB DIP

1 (6-ounce) can white crab meat, drained
1/4 cup mayonnaise
1 tablespoon catsup
8 ounces cream cheese, softened
2 tablespoons minced onion

Combine the crab meat, mayonnaise, catsup, cream cheese and onion in a bowl and mix well. Chill, covered, until serving time. Serve with bite-size fresh vegetables or crackers.

Yield: 12 to 15 servings

BAKED CRAB MEAT SPREAD

8 ounces cream cheese, softened
1 tablespoon milk
1 (7-ounce) can crab meat, drained
2 tablespoons grated onion
1 teaspoon prepared horseradish
1/4 teaspoon salt
pepper to taste
1/3 cup toasted slivered almonds

Preheat oven to 375 degrees. Mix the cream cheese and milk in a bowl until smooth. Add the crab meat, onion, horseradish, salt and pepper and mix well.

Spoon the crab meat mixture into a shallow baking dish. Sprinkle with the almonds. Bake for 15 minutes. Serve with crackers or corn chips.

Yield: 18 to 20 servings

PIZZA DIP

8 ounces cream cheese, softened
1 (14-ounce) jar pizza sauce
1/3 cup chopped onion
1 1/2 cups shredded mozzarella cheese
1 (6-ounce) can black olives, drained, chopped
2 ounces pepperoni slices, chopped

Preheat oven to 350 degrees. Spread the cream cheese in a 9-inch glass pie plate. Spread the pizza sauce over the cream cheese. Layer the onion, mozzarella cheese, olives and pepperoni over the pizza sauce. Bake for 25 minutes. Serve with light corn chips.

Yield: 30 servings

SPINACH DIP

1 (10-ounce) package frozen chopped spinach, drained
1 cup mayonnaise
1 cup sour cream
1/4 cup chopped green onions
1 envelope vegetable dip mix
chopped water chestnuts (optional)

Combine the spinach, mayonnaise, sour cream, green onions, dip mix and water chestnuts in a bowl and mix well. Chill, covered, for 2 hours. Serve in a hollowed-out bread bowl.

Yield: 25 to 30 servings

BLACK BEAN AND CORN SALSA

2 (15-ounce) cans black beans, rinsed, drained
2 (8-ounce) cans whole kernel corn, drained
1 (10-ounce) can tomatoes with green chiles, drained, chopped
1 small jar salsa
6 tablespoons vegetable oil
3 tablespoons lime juice
1 cup chopped fresh cilantro, or to taste
$1\frac{1}{2}$ teaspoons ground cumin

Combine the beans, corn, tomatoes with green chiles, salsa, oil, lime juice, cilantro and cumin in a bowl and mix well. Chill, covered, until serving time. Serve with corn chips or tortilla chips.
   Yield: 30 to 40 servings

 BLEU-STUFFED BRIE

$\frac{1}{2}$ cup crumbled bleu cheese
2 tablespoons toasted chopped walnuts
1 (8-ounce) wedge Brie, split into halves lengthwise

Mix the bleu cheese and walnuts in a small bowl. Spread over the cut surface of the bottom half of the Brie; replace the top half. Chill, tightly wrapped, for several hours. Preheat gas grill using medium setting. Unwrap the Brie and place on a square of heavy-duty foil or in a small baking pan. Grill for 10 minutes or until the Brie is softened. Serve with sourdough and French bread slices and apple and pear wedges.
   Yield: 6 to 8 servings

COUNTRY CAVIAR

3 cups cooked black-eyed peas, drained, rinsed
1 cup cooked rice
$1/2$ cup chopped green onions
$1/2$ cup vegetable oil
$3/4$ cup cider vinegar
$1/4$ cup sugar
1 teaspoon salt
1 to 2 teaspoons cayenne pepper
lettuce leaves

Combine the peas, rice, green onions, oil, vinegar, sugar, salt and cayenne in a bowl and mix well. Chill, covered, until serving time. Serve over lettuce. Garnish with chopped tomato and additional chopped green onions.

Yield: 8 to 10 servings

 CAFE BRULOT

1 orange
7 whole cloves
3 cinnamon sticks, broken into pieces
$3/4$ cup brandy
$1/4$ cup sugar
3 cups hot Louisiana coffee or dark roast coffee

Remove the orange peel in 1 continuous spiral, peeling off as much white pith as possible. Reserve the orange for another use. Combine the orange peel, cloves, cinnamon and brandy in a bowl or 2-cup measure. Let stand for 2 to 3 hours. Pour the brandy with the orange peel and spices over the sugar in a chafing dish. Ignite the brandy carefully. Pour in the hot coffee gradually to extinguish the flame. Ladle into demitasse cups.

Yield: 8 servings

HOT MOCHA MIX

3/4 cup hot cocoa mix
1/3 cup instant coffee
2 tablespoons nondairy creamer
4 teaspoons sugar
1/4 teaspoon cinnamon

Process the cocoa mix, coffee powder, creamer, sugar and cinnamon in a blender until mixed. To serve, measure 2 tablespoons of the mix into a mug and fill with boiling water.

Yield: 8 servings

BANANA FRUIT PUNCH

5 bananas, cut into large pieces
5 cups water
2 cups sugar
1 (12-ounce) can frozen orange juice concentrate
1 (6-ounce) can frozen lemon juice concentrate
1 (46-ounce) can unsweetened pineapple juice
1 (3-liter) bottle ginger ale

Process the bananas with just enough of the water to mix in a blender. Add the sugar, juice concentrates and pineapple juice and mix well. Pour into freezer containers. Freeze until needed. To serve, place the frozen mixture in a punch bowl and add the ginger ale. Thaw until slushy before serving.

Yield: 30 to 40 servings

COFFEE PUNCH

4 cups hot coffee
1 1/2 pints vanilla ice cream
nutmeg to taste

Pour the coffee over the ice cream in a bowl, stirring lightly until the ice cream is partially melted. Sprinkle with nutmeg.

Yield: 8 to 12 servings

HOT SPICED CRANBERRY PUNCH

1 gallon plus 2 cups cranberry juice
6 cups water
3 cups sugar
1 1/2 teaspoons cinnamon
1 teaspoon whole cloves
1 cup fresh lemon juice
1 1/2 cups orange juice
1/8 teaspoon salt, or to taste

Combine the cranberry juice, water, sugar, cinnamon and cloves in a large saucepan. Simmer for 15 minutes. Add the lemon juice, orange juice and salt. Bring to a boil; mix well and remove from the heat.

Yield: 50 servings

FRUIT PUNCH

2 cups sugar
2 cups water
1 (46-ounce) can orange juice
1 (46-ounce) can pineapple juice
2 (6-ounce) cans frozen lemonade concentrate, thawed
2 quarts ginger ale, chilled

Bring the sugar and water to a boil in a large saucepan. Remove from the heat. Chill until serving time. Stir in the orange juice, pineapple juice and lemonade concentrate. Stir in the ginger ale just before serving.
  Yield: 50 servings

PARTY PUNCH

2 quarts white grape juice, chilled
1 quart ginger ale, chilled

Combine the grape juice and ginger ale in a punch bowl and mix well. Serve immediately.
  Yield: 15 to 25 servings

SPICED PERCOLATOR PUNCH

1 tablespoon whole cloves
2$^1/_2$ cinnamon sticks
$^1/_8$ teaspoon salt, or to taste
1 (46-ounce) can pineapple juice
1 (64-ounce) bottle cranberry juice cocktail
3 cups water
$^3/_4$ cup packed brown sugar

Place the cloves, cinnamon stick and salt in the percolator basket. Mix the pineapple juice, cranberry juice cocktail, water and brown sugar in a large container; pour into the percolator. Perk using the manufacturer's directions. Serve hot.

Yield: 20 to 30 servings

PINEAPPLE SHERBET PUNCH

1 (46-ounce) can pineapple juice, chilled
3 cups chilled apricot nectar
1 quart club soda, chilled
1 quart pineapple sherbet

Combine the pineapple juice and apricot nectar in a large punch bowl. Add the club soda and sherbet just before serving.

Yield: 20 to 30 servings

PINEAPPLE AND LIME SHERBET PUNCH

1 (6-ounce) can frozen lemonade concentrate
1 (12-ounce) can frozen orange juice concentrate
3 cups pineapple juice
1 quart pineapple sherbet
1 quart lime sherbet
1 1/2 quarts ginger ale, chilled

Prepare the lemonade and orange juice using the package directions. Combine the lemonade and orange juice concentrates and pineapple juice in a large container. Chill for 2 hours. To serve, pour the juice mixture into a punch bowl. Add the pineapple sherbet and lime sherbet. Stir in the ginger ale.

Yield: 30 to 50 servings

WASSAIL

2 quarts apple juice
2 cups orange juice
1 cup lemon juice
1 (18-ounce) can pineapple juice
1 cinnamon stick
1 teaspoon (heaping) whole cloves
1/4 to 1/2 cup sugar

Combine the apple juice, orange juice, lemon juice, pineapple juice, cinnamon stick, cloves and sugar in a saucepan and mix well. Bring to a boil. Simmer, partially covered, for 1 hour. Serve hot.

Yield: 25 to 30 servings

CHAPTER TWO

SOUPS, SALADS AND BREADS

SHE-CRAB SOUP

1 quart milk
2 thin strips lemon peel
$^1/_4$ teaspoon nutmeg or mace
1 teaspoon salt
$^1/_8$ teaspoon hot pepper sauce
$^1/_4$ cup butter
4 to 6 saltines
2 cups blue crab meat with roe (about 6 to 7 boiled crabs)
dry sherry (optional)

Combine the milk, lemon peel and nutmeg in a heavy saucepan. Cook over very low heat until bubbles appear at the edge. Remove and discard the lemon peel.

Add the salt, hot pepper sauce and butter to the soup. Cook until the butter is melted, stirring occasionally.

Crumble in enough saltines to thicken the soup; mix well. Add the crab meat. Cook until heated through, stirring occasionally.

Pour a splash of sherry into each soup bowl. Ladle the soup into the bowls. Serve with additional saltines.

Chef's Note: Picking crab meat for She-Crab Soup is time-consuming but rewarding. First remove the legs; then lift the apron on the underside of the shell and break off. Lift out the body from the front. Remove the spongy fingers (also called "dead man"); then pick out the meat from the corners of the shell. Use a small fork to remove the roe (the red nuggets near the center of the body) and the white flakes of meat. Crack the claws and remove the meat.

Yield: 4 to 6 servings

OYSTER ARTICHOKE SOUP

2 quarts fresh oysters
2 pounds fresh mushrooms, cut into small pieces
3 cups whipping cream
1 pound butter roux (see Editor's Note)
1 No. 10 can artichokes (see Editor's Note)
3 onions, chopped
3 bunches green onions, chopped
1 bunch parsley, chopped
3 to 4 cups chicken stock
1$\frac{1}{2}$ tablespoons pepper
1$\frac{1}{2}$ tablespoons lemon juice
salt to taste
$\frac{1}{2}$ tablespoon rosemary
$\frac{1}{2}$ tablespoon thyme
$\frac{1}{2}$ tablespoon bay leaves

Scrub the oysters and rinse in cold water. Remove the oysters from the shell, holding them over a bowl to catch as much of the oyster liquid as possible. Set aside.

Combine the mushrooms, whipping cream, roux, artichokes, onions, green onions, parsley, chicken stock, pepper, lemon juice, salt, rosemary, thyme, bay leaves and reserved oyster liquid in a large stockpot and mix well.

Simmer over medium heat for 45 to 60 minutes or until the flavors have blended and the soup is heated through. Add the oysters just before serving time. Remove and discard the bay leaves. Ladle the soup into bowls.

Editor's Note: A roux is a mixture of flour and fat that can be used to thicken soups and sauces. Heat the butter in a separate pan or skillet; add flour to make the roux the desired consistency. Cook until the roux is dark golden brown, stirring constantly. A No. 10 can is a restaurant-size can with approximately a 12-cup volume.

Yield: 10 to 12 servings

SEAFOOD GUMBO BIG MAMOU

12 oysters
1/4 cup margarine
1 pound shrimp, peeled, deveined
1 cup coarsely chopped onion
3 cloves of garlic, chopped
1/4 cup chopped green bell pepper
1/4 cup chopped parsley
2 cups dark brown roux (see Editor's Note, page 33)
3 quarts hot water
1/2 teaspoon red pepper flakes
1/2 teaspoon white pepper
1 teaspoon black pepper
1/4 teaspoon thyme
1/4 teaspoon basil
1 bay leaf
1 teaspoon filé powder (optional)

Scrub the oysters and rinse in cold water. Remove the oysters from the shell, holding them over a bowl to catch as much of the oyster liquid as possible. Set aside.

Melt the margarine in a large saucepan. Add the shrimp and oysters. Sauté until the shrimp turn pink and the oysters are firm. Remove and set aside.

Sauté the onion, garlic, green pepper and parsley in the saucepan until tender. Add the roux gradually, stirring constantly. Add the reserved oyster liquid and enough of the hot water to make the gumbo the desired consistency; mix well.

Bring the gumbo to a rapid boil. Add the red pepper, white pepper, black pepper, thyme, basil, bay leaf, shrimp and oysters and mix well. Simmer for 18 minutes. Stir in the filé powder. Simmer for 2 minutes longer.

Remove and discard the bay leaf. Ladle the gumbo into deep soup bowls.
Yield: 6 servings

SEAFOOD PASTA CHOWDER

6 ounces miniature bow-tie pasta or other small shell pasta
6 tablespoons butter or margarine
8 ounces fresh mushrooms, cut into $1/8$-inch slices
2 (1-ounce) envelopes Newburg sauce mix
3 cups milk
$1^1/2$ cups water
$1/4$ cup dry white wine
$1/4$ cup finely chopped green onions
3 ounces frozen or canned crab meat

Cook the pasta using the package directions. Drain and rinse lightly with cold water to prevent the pasta from sticking together. Set aside.

Melt the butter in a 3-quart nonreactive heavy saucepan. Add the mushrooms. Sauté for 3 minutes. Add the sauce mix and mix well. Add the milk, water and wine and mix well.

Bring the chowder to a boil over medium heat, stirring constantly with a wire whisk. Reduce the heat. Simmer for 5 to 8 minutes, whisking constantly. Add the green onions, pasta and crab meat and mix well. Ladle into bowls. Garnish with parsley and serve immediately.

Editor's Note: See page 155 for the nutritional profile of this recipe.

Yield: 6 servings

BRUNSWICK STEW

1 pound boneless chicken breasts, skin removed, cut into 1-inch cubes
1 tablespoon olive oil
1 medium onion, chopped
$1^1/2$ cups chopped tomatoes
1 (6-ounce) can no-salt-added tomato paste
10 ounces each fresh or frozen baby lima beans and corn kernels
3 cups chicken stock
1 tablespoon Worcestershire sauce
3 tablespoons fresh lemon juice

Discard all visible fat from the chicken. Heat the olive oil in a deep skillet over medium-high heat. Add the onion. Sauté for 3 minutes or until tender. Stir in the chicken and remaining ingredients. Reduce the heat to low. Simmer, covered, for 1 hour. Editor's Note: See page 155 for the nutritional profile of this recipe.
  Yield: 8 servings

GARY'S CHICKEN SOUP

1 (3-pound) chicken including giblets, skin removed
2 to 3 celery tops, cut into 2-inch pieces
1 medium onion, chopped
2 carrots, cut into 2-inch pieces
1 teaspoon chicken bouillon
8 ounces small egg noodles
$^1/2$ teaspoon allspice
salt, pepper, sage and tarragon to taste

Combine the chicken with water to cover in a Dutch oven. Add the celery, onion and carrots. Boil until the chicken is cooked through. Strain the stock and set aside. Set aside a small amount of the giblets, celery, onion and carrots, discarding the remainder or reserving for another use. Debone and chop the chicken. Combine the stock, chicken, giblets, celery, onion, carrots, bouillon, noodles, allspice, salt, pepper, sage and tarragon in a large saucepan and mix well. Simmer for 4 hours. Editor's Note: See page 155 for the nutritional profile of this recipe.
  Yield: 6 servings

SPANISH CHICKEN SOUP

1 large fryer
4 quarts water
2 cloves of garlic
1 teaspoon celery seeds
2 teaspoons whole peppercorns
1 (16-ounce) can whole tomatoes
1 onion, coarsely chopped
1 green bell pepper, sliced
4 sprigs of parsley
1 teaspoon cumin
$1/4$ teaspoon cayenne pepper
1 teaspoon black pepper
1 clove of garlic, chopped
1 (10-ounce) package frozen corn kernels
5 green onions, chopped
salt to taste
1 cup cooked rice
2 teaspoons chopped parsley

Combine the chicken and water in a large stockpot. Tie 2 cloves of garlic, celery seeds and peppercorns in a cheesecloth bag; add to the stockpot. Cook, covered, until the chicken is tender. Remove the chicken from the broth and set aside.

Add the undrained tomatoes, onion, green pepper, parsley, cumin, cayenne pepper, black pepper and 1 clove of garlic to the broth. Simmer, covered, for 45 minutes. Add the corn, green onions and salt to the soup. Simmer for 15 minutes.

Remove and discard the chicken skin and bones. Chop the chicken into small pieces and add to the soup.

Add the rice and parsley to the soup and mix well. Simmer until heated through. Remove and discard the peppercorn mixture.

Yield: 12 to 15 servings

WHITE BEAN CHILI

2 pounds dried Great Northern beans
$3/4$ tablespoon ground cumin
1 tablespoon ground oregano
1 tablespoon onion salt
$1/2$ tablespoon cayenne pepper
$1/2$ tablespoon seasoning salt
4 pounds boneless skinless chicken breasts
$1/4$ cup vegetable oil
$1^1/2$ large onions, chopped
1 (27-ounce) can chopped mild green chiles
1 tablespoon minced garlic
1 gallon homemade or canned chicken stock
1 pint draft beer, or 1 (12-ounce) bottle beer

Rinse and sort the beans. Soak in water to cover overnight. Mix the cumin, oregano, onion salt, cayenne pepper and seasoning salt in a bowl.

Preheat oven to 350 degrees. Rinse the chicken and rub with half the spice mixture. Place in a baking pan. Bake for 15 minutes. Set aside.

Heat the oil in a skillet. Add the onions. Sauté until translucent. Add the green chiles, garlic and remaining spice mixture. Sauté for 1 minute.

Drain the beans and place in a large stockpot. Add the chicken stock, onion mixture and beer and mix well. Bring to a boil; reduce the heat. Simmer for 2 hours or until the beans are tender.

Cut the chicken into quarter-size pieces. Add to the soup. Simmer until the chicken is cooked through. Remove from the heat and ladle into bowls.

Yield: 10 to 12 servings

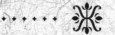

CANADIAN CHEESE SOUP

1 cup water
1 large potato, finely chopped
1 medium onion, finely chopped
$1/4$ cup finely chopped celery
$1/2$ cup finely chopped carrot
2 cups chicken broth
1 cup grated sharp Cheddar cheese
$1/2$ cup breakfast cream, evaporated milk or half-and-half
salt to taste
Tabasco sauce to taste

Bring the water to a boil in a $1^{1/2}$-quart saucepan. Add the potato, onion, celery and carrot; reduce the heat. Simmer, covered, for 15 to 20 minutes or until the vegetables are tender. Add the chicken broth, cheese, evaporated milk, salt and Tabasco sauce and mix well. Cook until heated through; do not boil.
  Yield: 4 to 6 servings

FRENCH ONION SOUP

4 large onions, chopped
$1/2$ cup butter or margarine
1 tablespoon flour
$1/2$ teaspoon paprika
1 teaspoon Worcestershire sauce
2 cups homemade chicken broth or beef broth
salt and pepper to taste
sliced French bread
grated Parmesan or Gruyère cheese

Sauté the onions in the butter in a large saucepan until translucent. Sprinkle with the flour, paprika and Worcestershire sauce. Sauté for 3 minutes. Add the broth. Bring to a boil. Season with salt and pepper. Simmer, covered, for 15 minutes. To serve, place 1 slice of French bread in each of 3 or 4 ovenproof soup bowls and cover with cheese. Fill the bowls with soup. Broil until the cheese is lightly browned.
  Yield: 3 to 4 servings

POTATO SOUP

2 cups chopped potatoes
1/2 cup chopped onion
1/2 cup chopped celery
3 cups chicken broth
5 tablespoons butter
3 tablespoons flour
3 cups hot milk
salt and pepper to taste

Cook the potatoes, onion and celery in the chicken broth in a saucepan until tender. Process in a blender until smooth. Melt the butter in a large saucepan. Add the flour, stirring until smooth. Add the milk gradually. Stir in the vegetable mixture. Season with salt and pepper. Simmer for 10 minutes.

Yield: 4 to 6 servings

POTATO CHEESE SOUP

1/2 cup butter
3/4 cup finely chopped onion
3/4 cup finely chopped carrot
2 cups chicken stock
1 tablespoon chopped parsley
1 large potato, peeled, cut into cubes
1 cup shredded Cheddar cheese
salt and pepper to taste

Melt the butter in a stockpot over medium heat. Add the onion and carrot. Sauté until tender. Add the chicken stock, parsley and potato. Cook until the potato is tender. Strain the vegetable mixture from the liquid, reserving the liquid. Purée the vegetable mixture in a blender or food processor. Return the vegetable mixture to the stockpot. Add the cheese. Cook until the cheese is melted, stirring constantly. Add the reserved liquid. Cook until of the desired consistency. Season with salt and pepper.

Yield: 4 servings

CREAM OF SPINACH SOUP

1 (10-ounce) package frozen chopped spinach, thawed
3 tablespoons flour
1 onion, chopped
1 cup evaporated milk
3 cups chicken broth
salt and pepper to taste

Purée the spinach, flour and onion in a blender. Add the evaporated milk and chicken broth. Process until smooth. Pour into a saucepan. Cook, covered, over low heat for 15 to 20 minutes or until heated through, stirring occasionally. Season with salt and pepper. Editor's Note: See page 155 for the nutritional profile of this recipe.

Yield: 4 servings

VICHYSQUASH SOUP

4 cups cooked squash
1 onion, chopped
1 cup chicken broth
1 teaspoon salt
$1/2$ teaspoon white pepper
2 tablespoons butter
1 cup sour cream
2 cups half-and-half

Purée the squash, onion, chicken broth, salt, pepper and butter in a food processor. Pour into a saucepan. Add the sour cream and half-and-half, beating with a wire whisk until mixed. Cook until heated through, stirring frequently; do not boil.

Yield: 6 to 8 servings

BLACK BEAN SALAD

2 (15-ounce) cans black beans, drained
2 tomatoes, seeded, chopped
1 bell pepper, chopped
4 green onions, chopped
2 tablespoons minced cilantro
2 tablespoons red wine vinegar
$1/2$ teaspoon each ground cumin and red pepper flakes
$1/4$ cup olive oil
salt and black pepper to taste
Bibb lettuce leaves
2 tablespoons chopped seeded tomato

Combine the beans, 2 tomatoes, bell pepper, green onions, cilantro, vinegar, cumin, red pepper, olive oil, salt and black pepper in a bowl and mix well. Chill, covered, for 1 hour. Serve over the lettuce. Top with 2 tablespoons tomato.

   Yield: 4 to 6 servings

KAREN'S SPECIALTY SALAD

1 head napa cabbage
1 bunch scallions
2 packages chicken ramen noodles
2 packages slivered almonds
2 tablespoons sesame seeds
$1/2$ cup sugar
$3/4$ cup olive oil
6 tablespoons white wine vinegar

Chop the cabbage and scallions to the consistency of cole slaw into a large bowl. Toast the noodles, almonds and sesame seeds on a baking sheet in the oven, breaking up the noodles. Mix the sugar, olive oil, contents of the flavor packets from the noodles and vinegar in a medium microwave-safe bowl. Microwave for 30 seconds or until heated through. Pour over the cabbage mixture and toss well.

   Yield: 6 to 8 servings

HOT GERMAN POTATO SALAD

5 medium potatoes
4 teaspoons vinegar
2 tablespoons vegetable oil
1/4 cup chopped onion
1 teaspoon caraway seeds
6 tablespoons mayonnaise
salt and pepper to taste

Cook the potatoes in water to cover in a saucepan until tender; drain well. Peel and dice the potatoes. Combine with the vinegar and oil in a large bowl. Add the onion, caraway seeds and mayonnaise and mix well. Season with salt and pepper. Serve hot.

Yield: 4 to 6 servings

CREOLE TOMATO SALAD

3 tablespoons salad oil
3 tablespoons vinegar
1 teaspoon salt
1/4 teaspoon prepared mustard
1/4 teaspoon white pepper
1/4 teaspoon red pepper flakes
4 large Creole tomatoes, chopped
2 cucumbers, sliced
2 mild jalapeños, chopped
1 onion, thinly sliced
1/4 cup finely chopped celery
1 cup crumbled feta cheese or other similar cheese

Combine the salad oil, vinegar, salt, mustard, white pepper and red pepper in a bowl and whisk until creamy. Combine the tomatoes, cucumbers, jalapeños, onion, celery and cheese in a salad bowl. Add the dressing and toss lightly.

Yield: 6 servings

SPINACH SALAD

1 package spinach, torn into bite-size pieces
1 cup bean sprouts
1 (8-ounce) can sliced water chestnuts, drained
3 hard-cooked eggs, chopped
6 slices bacon, crisp-cooked, crumbled
1 cup vegetable oil
$1/2$ cup vinegar
$1/2$ small onion, grated
$3/4$ cup sugar
$1/3$ cup catsup
2 tablespoons Worcestershire sauce
salt to taste

Mix the spinach, bean sprouts, water chestnuts, eggs and bacon in a salad bowl. Combine the oil, vinegar, onion, sugar, catsup, Worcestershire sauce and salt in a jar with a tight-fitting lid and shake well to mix. Pour over the salad and toss lightly.
   Yield: 3 to 4 servings

SPINACH AND CHEESE SALAD

2 (10-ounce) packages frozen spinach, cooked, drained
$1/2$ cup each chopped celery and onion
1 cup chopped Old English cheese
2 hard-cooked eggs, chopped
$1/2$ teaspoon Tabasco sauce
$1 1/2$ teaspoons wine vinegar
$1/2$ teaspoon salt
$1 1/4$ cups mayonnaise

Combine the spinach, celery, onion, cheese and eggs in a salad bowl and mix well. Mix the Tabasco sauce, vinegar, salt and mayonnaise in a small bowl. Fold into the spinach mixture. Chill, covered, until serving time.
   Yield: 6 to 8 servings

MARINATED ORIENTAL SALAD

1 (16-ounce) can bean sprouts, drained
1 (12-ounce) can Shoe Peg corn, drained
1 (17-ounce) can tiny green peas, drained
1 (8-ounce) can sliced water chestnuts, drained
1 each green bell pepper and onion, thinly sliced
1 cup each vegetable oil, water and sugar
$1/2$ cup vinegar
$1/2$ teaspoon paprika
seasoned salt and coarsely ground pepper to taste

Combine the bean sprouts, corn, peas, water chestnuts, green pepper and onion in a salad bowl. Mix the remaining ingredients in a bowl. Pour over the salad and toss lightly. Chill, covered, for 24 to 48 hours. Drain well before serving.

Yield: 10 servings

MOTHER'S CRANBERRY SALAD RING

4 (3-ounce) packages black raspberry gelatin
2 cups boiling water
$1/2$ cup cold water
2 cups fresh cranberries, ground
2 large unpeeled oranges, seeded, ground
2 unpeeled apples, cored, ground
1 (16-ounce) can crushed pineapple
2 cups sugar
1 cup chopped pecans

Dissolve the gelatin in the boiling water in a large bowl. Stir in the cold water. Chill, covered, until partially set. Mix the cranberries, oranges, apples, undrained pineapple, sugar and pecans in a bowl. Fold into the fruit mixture. Spoon into a lightly oiled 10-cup ring mold. Chill until set. Garnish each serving with lettuce leaves, orange slices or mayonnaise. Editor's Note: See page 155 for the nutritional profile of this recipe.

Yield: 18 servings

SIMPLE PASTA SALAD

8 ounces small seashell pasta
1 (10-ounce) package frozen mixed vegetables
1 small red onion, chopped
$1/2$ cup chopped celery
$1/2$ to 1 cup mayonnaise or mayonnaise-type salad dressing
salt and pepper to taste

Add the pasta and mixed vegetables to a large saucepan of boiling water; return to a boil. Boil for 12 minutes or until tender; drain and rinse with cold water. Combine the cooled pasta, mixed vegetables, onion, celery, mayonnaise, salt and pepper in a large bowl and mix well. The salad may be served as soon as prepared but is better if chilled overnight. Editor's Note: See page 155 for the nutritional profile of this recipe.
   Yield: 8 servings

WEST INDIES SALAD

1 medium onion, chopped
1 pound fresh lump crab meat, flaked
salt and pepper to taste
$1/2$ cup vegetable oil
$1/2$ cup cider vinegar
6 tablespoons ice water

Spread half the onion in a bowl. Cover with the crab meat; top with the remaining onion. Sprinkle with salt and pepper. Mix the oil, vinegar and ice water in a bowl. Pour over the salad. Chill, covered, overnight.
   Yield: 2 to 4 servings

• • • • • • • • • • • • • • • • ❈ • • • • • • • • • • • • • • • •

SALMON SALAD

4 (1-inch-thick) salmon steaks
1/4 cup vegetable oil
1/4 cup lemon juice
1 tablespoon water
1 tablespoon soy sauce
2 teaspoons sesame oil
2 teaspoons honey
4 cups shredded mixed salad greens
1/4 cup chopped green onions
1/2 cup alfalfa sprouts
1 banana, chopped (optional)
1 tablespoon toasted sesame seeds
pepper to taste

Place the salmon in a sealable plastic bag in a shallow dish. Mix the vegetable oil, lemon juice, water, soy sauce, sesame oil and honey in a bowl.

Pour the honey mixture over the fish; seal the bag. Marinate in the refrigerator for 6 hours, turning the bag occasionally.

Preheat gas grill using medium to high setting. Remove the fish from the marinade; place the remaining marinade in a saucepan.

Place the fish on a greased grid. Grill for 10 to 12 minutes or until the fish flakes easily, turning once. Heat the marinade until bubbly.

Mix the salad greens, green onions, alfalfa sprouts, banana, sesame seeds and pepper in a salad bowl. To serve, pour the hot marinade over the greens and toss lightly to wilt. Top with the grilled salmon.

Yield: 4 servings

SALMON CAESAR SALAD

1/4 cup olive oil or vegetable oil

2 tablespoons white wine vinegar

1 clove of garlic, minced

2 anchovy fillets, mashed

1/8 teaspoon pepper, or to taste

2 (1-pound) salmon fillets

1 bunch romaine lettuce, torn into bite-size pieces

1 cup unseasoned croutons

1/4 cup grated Parmesan cheese

Preheat gas grill using medium setting. Mix the olive oil, vinegar, garlic, anchovies and pepper in a small bowl. Brush over both sides of the salmon. Grill for 10 minutes per side or until the fish flakes easily, brushing occasionally with the olive oil mixture. Separate the salmon into bite-size pieces. Combine the salmon, lettuce, croutons, cheese and remaining olive oil mixture in a large bowl and toss lightly.

Editor's Note: See page 155 for the nutritional profile of this recipe.

    Yield: 4 servings

TUNA CABBAGE SALAD

1 (6-ounce) can tuna, drained

2 cups finely chopped cabbage

2 tablespoons (about) mayonnaise

1/2 small onion, chopped

1/4 teaspoon salt

1/8 teaspoon pepper (optional)

1 1/2 to 2 tablespoons sweet or sour pickle relish, or to taste

Combine the tuna, cabbage, mayonnaise, onion, salt, pepper and pickle relish in a large bowl and mix well. Chill, covered, for several hours. The cabbage will become soggy unless served within a few hours of preparation.

    Yield: 2 to 3 servings

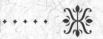

BAKED APPLE PANCAKE

3 tablespoons sugar
$3/4$ teaspoon ground cinnamon
2 tablespoons butter or margarine
1 large apple, peeled, sliced
4 eggs
$2/3$ cup milk
$1/3$ cup flour
1 tablespoon sugar
$1/2$ teaspoon salt
confectioners' sugar

Combine 3 tablespoons sugar and cinnamon in a bowl and mix well. Heat the butter in a 10-inch oven-proof skillet until melted. Sprinkle with the sugar mixture.

Arrange the apple slices over the sugar mixture. Cook over medium-low heat for 3 to 4 minutes or just until heated through. Remove from the heat and let cool.

Preheat oven to 400 degrees. Beat the eggs, milk, flour, 1 tablespoon sugar and salt in a large bowl until smooth. Spoon over the apple slices.

Bake for 15 minutes or until the pancake is golden brown and the side is puffy. Sprinkle with confectioners' sugar. Serve immediately.

Yield: 4 to 6 servings

FRUIT AND YOGURT COFFEE CAKE

1 (6-ounce) package dried fruit bits
1/2 cup butter, softened
1 cup sugar
2 eggs
1 cup vanilla yogurt
2 cups flour
1 teaspoon baking powder
1 teaspoon baking soda
1/2 teaspoon cinnamon
1/4 teaspoon salt
1/2 cup chopped pecans or walnuts
1/4 cup sugar
1/2 teaspoon cinnamon

Soak the dried fruit in hot water to cover for 10 minutes; drain well and set aside. Cream the butter and 1 cup sugar in a mixer bowl until light and fluffy. Beat in the eggs 1 at a time. Blend in the yogurt.

Sift the flour, baking powder, baking soda, 1/2 teaspoon cinnamon and salt into the creamed mixture and mix well. Stir in the fruit. Spoon into a greased 9x13-inch baking pan.

Mix the pecans, 1/4 cup sugar and 1/2 teaspoon cinnamon in a small bowl. Sprinkle over the batter. Chill, covered, for 8 hours or longer. Preheat oven to 350 degrees. Bake for 30 to 35 minutes or until the coffee cake tests done.

Editor's Note: See page 155 for the nutritional profile of this recipe.
Yield: 16 servings

ALABAMA CORN MUFFINS

1½ cups melted margarine
3 cups cornmeal
2 cups flour
¾ cup sugar
1½ teaspoons salt
½ teaspoon baking soda
1 tablespoon baking powder
2¼ cups (or more) buttermilk
¾ cup milk
3 medium eggs
½ cup cream-style corn

Preheat oven to 350 degrees. Brush some of the melted margarine into muffin cups. Heat the muffin cups in the oven. Keep the remaining margarine warm in a saucepan over low heat.

Combine the cornmeal, flour, sugar, salt, baking soda and baking powder in a large bowl and mix well. Make a well in the center of the dry ingredients.

Add 2¼ cups buttermilk, milk, eggs and corn to the well, stirring to form a batter and adding additional buttermilk if needed.

Stir the warm margarine into the batter. Spoon the batter into the hot muffin cups. Bake for 20 to 25 minutes or until the muffins are golden brown and a wooden pick inserted near the center comes out clean.

Remove the muffins from the oven. Let stand for 5 minutes before removing from the muffin cups. Serve with Peach Butter (see page 56).

Yield: 1½ dozen

MAYONNAISE MUFFINS

1 cup self-rising flour
1/2 cup milk
1/4 cup mayonnaise

Preheat oven to 450 degrees. Mix the flour, milk and mayonnaise in a bowl. Spoon into 12 small or 6 large lightly greased muffin cups. Bake for 12 to 15 minutes or until browned. Serve with honey butter.

Yield: 1 dozen

GOLDEN OATMEAL MUFFINS

1 cup sifted flour
1 tablespoon baking powder
1/2 teaspoon salt
1/4 cup sugar
1 cup rolled oats
3 tablespoons vegetable oil
1 egg, beaten
1 cup milk

Preheat oven to 425 degrees. Sift the flour, baking powder, salt and sugar into a bowl. Stir in the oats. Add the oil, egg and milk, stirring just until moistened. Fill greased medium muffin cups 2/3 full with batter. Bake for 15 minutes or until golden brown. Serve hot.

Yield: 1 dozen

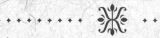

PUMPKIN AND OAT BRAN MUFFINS

1½ cups oat bran
⅔ cup packed brown sugar
½ cup flour
2 teaspoons baking powder
1 teaspoon pumpkin pie spice
¼ teaspoon salt
1 cup mashed cooked pumpkin
½ cup skim milk
2 egg whites, beaten
2 tablespoons vegetable oil

Preheat oven to 425 degrees. Spray muffin cups with nonstick cooking spray. Mix the oat bran, brown sugar, flour, baking powder, pie spice and salt in a bowl. Make a well in the center of the mixture. Add the pumpkin, skim milk, egg whites and oil, stirring just until moistened. Fill the muffin cups ⅔ full with batter. Bake for 20 minutes. Remove from the pan immediately.

Yield: 1 dozen

GARLIC BISCUITS

⅓ cup melted margarine or butter
¼ teaspoon garlic powder
⅛ teaspoon pepper, or to taste
1 (10-count) can refrigerator buttermilk biscuits

Preheat gas grill using medium setting. Mix the margarine, garlic powder and pepper in a small bowl. Pat each biscuit into a 3-inch round; brush each side with the margarine mixture. Grill for 4 to 5 minutes per side or until golden brown. Serve with additional margarine if desired.

Yield: 10 servings

PRALINE BISCUITS

36 pecan halves
$1/2$ cup margarine
$1/2$ cup packed light brown sugar
1 tablespoon cinnamon
2 cups buttermilk baking mix
$1/3$ cup milk
$1/3$ cup applesauce

Preheat oven to 200 degrees. Place 3 pecan halves, 2 teaspoons margarine, 2 teaspoons brown sugar and $1/4$ teaspoon cinnamon in each of 12 muffin cups. Heat in warm oven until the margarine is melted. Remove from the oven. Increase oven temperature to 450 degrees. Combine the baking mix, milk and applesauce in a bowl; beat for 20 strokes. Spoon into the muffin cups. Bake for 10 minutes. Invert onto a serving plate.

Yield: 1 dozen

SEEDED ROLLS

1 package brown-and-serve rolls
2 tablespoons melted butter or margarine
$1/4$ teaspoon onion salt
$1/2$ teaspoon sesame seeds, poppy seeds, caraway seeds or celery seeds

Preheat oven using roll package directions. Place the rolls on a baking sheet. Brush the tops with the butter. Sprinkle each with onion salt and sesame seeds. Bake using the package directions.

Yield: 1 dozen

TWO-CORN BREAD

1 cup flour
1 cup yellow cornmeal
2 tablespoons sugar
1 tablespoon baking powder
$1/4$ teaspoon salt
3 eggs
1 cup cream-style cottage cheese
1 (8-ounce) can cream-style corn

Preheat oven to 375 degrees. Mix the flour, cornmeal, sugar, baking powder and salt in a large bowl. Beat the eggs and cottage cheese in a medium bowl until smooth. Stir in the corn. Add to the flour mixture, stirring just until mixed. Spoon into a greased 9x9-inch baking pan. Bake for 30 to 35 minutes or until golden brown. Serve warm.

Yield: 9 servings

ROSEMARY GARLIC BREAD

$1/2$ cup margarine or butter, softened
2 tablespoons chopped parsley
2 cloves of garlic, minced
$1/2$ teaspoon dried rosemary
1 (16-ounce) loaf Italian or French bread

Preheat gas grill using medium setting. Mix the margarine, parsley, garlic and rosemary in a small bowl. Cut the bread into halves lengthwise. Spread the margarine mixture over each cut surface; reassemble the loaf. Wrap the bread tightly in heavy-duty foil. Grill for 15 to 20 minutes or until heated through, turning occasionally. Cut into 1-inch slices to serve.

Yield: 12 to 14 servings

CRANBERRY BREAD

2 cups sifted flour
$1/2$ teaspoon baking soda
$1^1/2$ teaspoons baking powder
1 teaspoon salt
1 cup sugar
grated peel and juice of 1 orange
2 tablespoons shortening
1 egg, beaten
1 cup chopped pecans or walnuts
1 cup cranberries, cut into quarters

Sift the flour, baking soda, baking powder and salt into a medium bowl. Add the sugar. Mix the orange peel, orange juice and shortening in a large glass measure. Add enough boiling water to measure $3/4$ cup. Combine the orange juice mixture and egg in a large bowl. Add the flour mixture and mix well. Stir in the pecans and cranberries. Spoon into a greased and floured loaf pan. Let stand for 20 minutes. Preheat oven to 350 degrees. Bake for 1 hour and 10 minutes.
Yield: 10 to 12 servings

PEACH BUTTER

1 pound butter, softened
$1/4$ cup chopped peaches
1 teaspoon peach schnapps

Combine the butter, peaches and peach schnapps in a bowl and mix well. Shape into a log. Freeze, tightly wrapped with plastic wrap, until firm. Cut into thin slices to serve. Spread on hot corn bread or biscuits.
Yield: 1 pound

CHAPTER THREE

MEAT AND POULTRY ENTREES

❖ ❖

STUFFED WAGON WHEEL BURGER

2 pounds ground chuck
1 teaspoon salt
$1/4$ teaspoon pepper
1 egg, beaten
1 cup herb-seasoned stuffing mix, slightly crushed
1 (4-ounce) can mushroom stems and pieces, drained, chopped
$1/3$ cup beef broth or beef bouillon
$1/4$ cup sliced green onions
$1/4$ cup chopped parsley
2 tablespoons melted butter

Preheat gas grill using medium setting. Combine the ground chuck, salt and pepper in a bowl and mix well. Divide into 2 equal portions. Flatten each portion into an 8-inch round on waxed paper.

Combine the egg, stuffing mix, mushrooms, beef broth, green onions, parsley and butter in a bowl and mix lightly. Spoon over 1 round to within 1 inch of the edge. Top with the remaining round, pressing the edges together. Grill in a wire basket for 20 minutes or until cooked through, turning once.

Yield: 8 servings

SKILLET SPAGHETTI

1 pound ground beef
1 large onion, chopped
1 (48-ounce) jar spaghetti sauce
1 (7-ounce) package thin spaghetti, broken into pieces
1 (4-ounce) can mushroom stems and pieces, drained
$1/2$ cup water
1 tablespoon sugar
$1/2$ teaspoon salt

Brown the ground beef with the onion in a 4-quart Dutch oven, stirring until the ground beef is crumbly; drain well. Stir in the spaghetti sauce, spaghetti, mushrooms, water, sugar and salt. Bring to a boil; reduce the heat. Simmer, covered, for 25 minutes or until the spaghetti is tender, stirring occasionally.

   Yield: 6 servings

SKILLET STROGANOFF

1 pound ground beef
1 medium onion, chopped
1 (10-ounce) can beef broth
1 (4-ounce) can mushroom stems and pieces, drained
4 ounces egg noodles
$1^1/2$ cups water
$1/4$ cup catsup
$1/4$ teaspoon garlic powder
1 cup sour cream

Brown the ground beef with the onion in a 10-inch skillet, stirring until the ground beef is crumbly; drain well. Stir in the beef broth, mushrooms, noodles, water, catsup and garlic powder. Bring to a boil; reduce the heat. Simmer, covered, for 30 minutes or until the noodles are tender, stirring occasionally and adding a small amount of water if needed. Stir in the sour cream. Cook just until hot.

   Yield: 5 servings

BARBECUE CUPS

12 ounces ground beef
$1/2$ cup barbecue sauce
$1/4$ cup chopped onion
2 tablespoons brown sugar
1 (8-ounce) can refrigerator biscuits
$3/4$ cup shredded Cheddar cheese

Preheat oven to 400 degrees. Brown the ground beef in a large skillet, stirring until crumbly; drain. Stir in the barbecue sauce, onion and brown sugar; set aside. Separate the biscuit dough into layers. Line each of 12 ungreased muffin cups with equal amounts of biscuit layers. Spoon the ground beef mixture into the muffin cups. Sprinkle each with cheese. Bake for 10 to 12 minutes or until bubbly.

   Yield: 12 servings

DEEP-DISH PIZZA

1 pound ground beef
1 medium onion, chopped
1 small bell pepper, chopped
1 (16-ounce) can tomatoes, drained
1 package pepperoni pizza mix
$1/2$ cup warm water
2 cups shredded mozzarella cheese

Cook the ground beef, onion and bell pepper in a skillet until the onion and bell pepper are tender, stirring until the ground beef is crumbly; drain well. Stir in the tomatoes and the pizza sauce from the packaged pizza mix. Simmer for 15 minutes. Preheat oven to 425 degrees. Mix the pizza dough and warm water in a small bowl. Spread the dough in a greased 9x13-inch baking pan. Spread the ground beef mixture over the dough. Sprinkle with the cheese. Bake for 20 to 30 minutes or until the crust is browned. Let cool for 10 minutes.

   Yield: 4 to 6 servings

GROUND BEEF CASSEROLE

1 (15-ounce) can chopped tomatoes
1 pound ground beef
1 large onion, chopped
1 clove of garlic, minced
$1/3$ cup soy sauce
$1\frac{1}{2}$ teaspoons chili powder
2 cups elbow macaroni
4 ounces medium-sharp Cheddar cheese, grated

Preheat oven to 350 degrees. Drain the tomatoes, reserving the liquid. Mix the liquid with enough water to measure 3 cups. Cook the ground beef, onion and garlic in a skillet until the onion and garlic are tender, stirring until the ground beef is crumbly; drain well. Stir in the reserved liquid, tomatoes, soy sauce and chili powder. Cook just until boiling. Place the macaroni and the cheese in a 7x11-inch baking dish. Add the ground beef mixture and stir gently. Bake for 30 minutes or until the macaroni is al dente, stirring once.

Yield: 6 to 8 servings

TEXAS HASH

3 tablespoons vegetable oil
2 green bell peppers, sliced
2 large onions, sliced
1 pound ground beef
2 cups cooked tomatoes
1 cup cooked rice
1 teaspoon each chili powder and salt
$1/8$ teaspoon pepper, or to taste
buttered bread crumbs or cracker crumbs

Preheat oven to 350 degrees. Heat the oil in a skillet. Add the green pepper and onions. Sauté until tender. Add the ground beef. Cook until the ground beef is browned, stirring until crumbly; drain well. Add the tomatoes, rice, chili powder, salt and pepper and mix well. Spoon into a greased baking dish. Top with bread crumbs. Bake until the crumbs are golden brown.

Yield: 4 to 6 servings

BLEU CHEESE MEATBALL KABOBS

12 large mushroom caps
1 cup dry white wine or chicken broth
1 1/2 pounds lean ground beef
1/2 cup crumbled bleu cheese
2 tablespoons chopped green onions
1 egg
1/2 teaspoon salt
1/8 teaspoon pepper
18 small pitted olives

Marinate the mushrooms in the wine in a shallow glass dish for 1 hour. Remove the mushrooms from the marinade, discarding the remaining marinade. Preheat gas grill using medium setting. Mix the ground beef, cheese, green onions, egg, salt and pepper in a large bowl. Shape 1 meatball around each olive. Thread 3 meatballs and 2 mushrooms alternately on each of 6 skewers. Grill for 20 minutes or until the meatballs are cooked through, turning occasionally.

Yield: 4 to 6 servings

STEAK MAYON STYLE

1 1/2 pounds chuck steak or round steak, cut into strips
juice of 1 orange
2 tablespoons lemon juice
butter
3/4 teaspoon garlic salt
1 medium onion, chopped
2 tomatoes, sliced
1/2 bell pepper, chopped

Marinate the steak in a mixture of the orange juice and lemon juice for 30 minutes. Remove the steak from the marinade, reserving the remaining marinade. Brown the steak in butter in a skillet. Pour the reserved marinade over the steak. Simmer for 30 minutes. Add the garlic salt, onion, tomatoes and bell pepper. Cook until the vegetables are tender, stirring occasionally.

Yield: 4 to 6 servings

CARPETBAG STEAK

2 pounds sirloin steak, 1½ inches thick
8 oysters
salt and pepper to taste
melted butter
1 teaspoon lemon juice
1 teaspoon chopped parsley

Preheat broiler. Make a slit in the center of the steak to form a pocket. Season the oysters with salt and pepper and insert into the pocket. Brush the steak with butter. Place on a rack in a broiler pan. Broil to desired degree of doneness. Mix the lemon juice and chopped parsley with the pan drippings. Pour the mixture over the steak.

   Yield: 4 to 6 servings

GRILLED MUSTARD STEAK

1 sirloin steak, 1 inch thick
2 tablespoons prepared mustard
2 tablespoons butter, softened

Trim any excess fat from the edge of the steak. Slash the remaining fat at 1-inch intervals. Brush the steak with a mixture of the mustard and butter. Let stand for 30 minutes. Preheat gas grill using medium setting. Grill to desired degree of doneness.

   Yield: 1 to 2 servings

🔥 ROQUEFORT FLANK STEAK

2 ounces Roquefort cheese, crumbled
1/4 cup thinly sliced green onions
2 cloves of garlic, minced
1/4 teaspoon hot pepper sauce
1/4 teaspoon pepper
1 (1 1/2-pound) flank steak

Preheat gas grill using medium setting. Mix the cheese, green onions, garlic, hot pepper sauce and pepper in a bowl. Grill the steak for 10 to 15 minutes for medium, turning once. Spoon the garlic mixture over the steak during the last 5 minutes cooking time. Editor's Note: See page 155 for the nutritional profile of this recipe.

Yield: 6 servings

🔥 PEPPERED RIB-EYE STEAKS

1/4 cup minced parsley
2 tablespoons finely chopped shallots
4 cloves of garlic, minced
2 tablespoons crushed white peppercorns
1 tablespoon crushed black peppercorns
4 rib-eye steaks, fat trimmed

Mix the parsley, shallots, garlic, white peppercorns and black peppercorns in a bowl. Rub on both sides of each steak. Chill, covered, for 1 hour. Preheat gas grill using medium setting. Grill the steaks for 10 minutes for medium, turning once.

Yield: 4 servings

⚘ SAUSAGE MUSHROOM SIRLOIN STEAK

8 ounces lean ground pork
1 cup sliced mushrooms
1/2 cup chopped onion
2 cloves of garlic, minced
1/2 teaspoon dried rosemary
1/2 teaspoon dried thyme
1/2 teaspoon salt
1/4 teaspoon pepper
1 (2-pound) sirloin steak, with pocket for stuffing

Preheat gas grill using medium setting. Sauté the ground pork, mushrooms, onion, garlic, rosemary and thyme in a medium skillet over medium-low flame until the pork is cooked through; drain well. Stir in the salt and pepper. Spoon the pork mixture into the steak pocket; secure the edges with small metal skewers. Grill for 12 to 15 minutes for medium, turning once.

Yield: 6 to 8 servings

⚘ STEAK AND SHRIMP CAESAR

3/4 cup creamy Caesar salad dressing
4 sirloin steaks, fat trimmed
1/4 cup finely chopped red bell pepper
1/4 cup finely chopped green onions
1 tablespoon vegetable oil
12 large shrimp

Pour the salad dressing over the steaks in a shallow glass dish. Marinate in the refrigerator for 1 to 2 hours, turning occasionally. Remove the steaks from the marinade, reserving the remaining marinade. Preheat gas grill using medium setting. Sauté the red pepper and green onions in the oil in a small skillet over medium flame until tender; set aside. Thread 3 shrimp on each of 4 metal skewers. Place the shrimp and steaks on the grill. Grill for 10 minutes for medium steaks, turning once and basting frequently with the reserved marinade. Serve the shrimp kabobs over the steaks. Sprinkle with the green onion mixture.

Yield: 4 servings

GERALD'S FILLET OF BEEF

1 cup sliced mushrooms
1/2 cup chopped leeks
1/2 cup port
1 (5-ounce) round fillet of beef
Brown Rosemary Sauce

Cook the mushrooms and leeks in the wine in a skillet until tender; drain well. Spread the mushroom mixture over the fillet. Roll up the fillet, securing with a wooden pick or kitchen string. Cook the fillet in the skillet to desired degree of doneness. Serve Brown Rosemary Sauce over the fillet.

Yield: 1 serving

BROWN ROSEMARY SAUCE

2 tablespoons chopped rosemary
3 tomatoes, chopped
1 (12-ounce) can tomato juice
1 rib celery, chopped
2 large onions, chopped
4 large carrots, chopped
2 tablespoons chopped thyme
1 cup sliced mushrooms
3 ounces beef stock
cornstarch

Combine the rosemary, tomatoes, tomato juice, celery, onions, carrots, thyme, mushrooms and beef stock in a saucepan. Boil for 1 hour. Strain the stock through a sieve. Return the strained stock to the saucepan. Cook until heated through, stirring in a small amount of cornstarch at a time until of the desired consistency.

OLD NO. 7 TENNESSEE BEEF BRISKET

1 (4- to 6-pound) beef brisket
1/4 cup Jack Daniel's whiskey
1/4 cup soy sauce
1 medium onion, finely chopped
2 cloves of garlic, minced
2 tablespoons Dijon mustard
1/4 cup catsup (optional)
1/8 teaspoon Worcestershire sauce, or to taste
1/4 cup packed brown sugar
pepper to taste

Trim the external fat on the brisket to 1/4 inch. Place the brisket in a sealable plastic bag or shallow glass dish. Mix the whiskey, soy sauce, onion, garlic, Dijon mustard, catsup, Worcestershire sauce, brown sugar and pepper in a bowl. Add enough water to measure 2 cups marinade. Pour the marinade over the brisket. Seal or cover tightly. Chill for 8 hours to overnight.

Preheat oven to 275 degrees. Remove the brisket from the marinade, reserving the remaining marinade. Place the brisket on a baking sheet lined with heavy-duty foil or in a foil roasting pan. Pour the reserved marinade over the brisket. Cover with heavy-duty foil and seal tightly. Bake for 4 to 5 hours or to desired degree of doneness. Remove the brisket from the pan, reserving the pan drippings.

Preheat gas grill using medium setting. Place the brisket fat side down on the grill; close the grill lid. Cook for 30 minutes.

Skim the fat from the reserved pan drippings. Reheat the pan drippings in a saucepan. Serve with the brisket.

Editor's Note: To add a hickory-smoked flavor, soak hickory chips in water for 30 minutes. Wrap the chips in foil and place on the briquets while the meat is grilling.

Yield: 12 to 18 servings

❦ BEEF ROAST WITH JALAPENO CORN BREAD STUFFING

1 (4-pound) boneless sirloin tip roast
Jalapeño Corn Bread Stuffing

Untie the roast and unroll on a cutting board. Spoon Jalapeño Corn Bread Stuffing onto the roast; roll up and tie in several places with kitchen string. Preheat gas grill using medium setting. Place a disposable foil pan in the center of the grill under the grids. Place the roast in the center of the grill. Grill for 1 hour and 40 minutes for medium or until a meat thermometer registers 160 degrees. Editor's Note: See page 155 for the nutritional profile of this recipe.

Yield: 10 servings

JALAPENO CORN BREAD STUFFING

$^1/_2$ cup chopped onion
$^1/_2$ cup chopped red bell pepper
1 to 2 fresh or canned jalapeño peppers, finely chopped
1 tablespoon vegetable oil
$^1/_2$ (8-ounce) package corn bread stuffing
$^1/_4$ cup water
1 egg, beaten

Sauté the onion, red pepper and jalapeño pepper in the oil in a small skillet over medium flame until tender. Combine with the corn bread stuffing in a large bowl and mix well. Add the water and egg, tossing to mix.

MONGOLIAN BEEF

$1/2$ cup soy sauce
1 tablespoon dry sherry
2 teaspoons sesame oil
3 tablespoons cornstarch
2 tablespoons brown sugar
2 teaspoons crushed red pepper
4 to 6 dried whole red peppers
1 (2-pound) boneless sirloin tip roast, thinly sliced
2 tablespoons vegetable oil
4 bunches green onions, sliced
$1/4$ cup vegetable oil

Mix the soy sauce, sherry, sesame oil, cornstarch, brown sugar, crushed red pepper and whole red peppers in a large bowl. Add the beef. Marinate, covered, in the refrigerator for 20 minutes. Remove the grate from 1 side of a gas grill. Preheat using medium-high setting. Heat a wok on the briquettes. Add 2 tablespoons oil and the green onions. Stir-fry for 5 minutes. Remove the onions. Add $1/4$ cup oil. Heat for 1 minute. Add the beef mixture. Stir-fry until the beef is cooked through. Return the onions to the wok. Stir-fry for 1 minute. Serve over rice.

Yield: 6 to 8 servings

GRILLED POT ROAST

1 (2- to 3-pound) pot roast
1 envelope onion soup mix
1 (10-ounce) can cream of mushroom soup

Preheat gas grill using low setting. Place the roast on a large sheet of double-thickness heavy-duty foil. Sprinkle the onion soup mix over the roast. Spoon the mushroom soup over the top. Fold the foil to form an airtight packet. Grill with the lid open for 3 hours or to desired degree of doneness.

Yield: 4 to 6 servings

CHUCK WAGON ROAST

1 (4-pound) boneless chuck roast, fat trimmed
1 (12-ounce) can beer
2 tablespoons Worcestershire sauce
3 tablespoons vegetable oil
1/4 cup packed light brown sugar
1 teaspoon onion powder
1 teaspoon garlic powder
1/2 teaspoon salt
1/2 teaspoon pepper

Pierce the roast several times with a long-tined fork; place in a shallow glass dish. Mix the beer, Worcestershire sauce, oil, brown sugar, onion powder, garlic powder, salt and pepper in a bowl; pour over the roast. Marinate, covered, in the refrigerator for 8 hours to overnight, turning occasionally. Remove the roast from the marinade, reserving the remaining marinade. Preheat gas grill using medium setting. Grill the roast for 1 hour to 1 hour and 15 minutes for medium, turning occasionally and basting with reserved marinade. Remove the roast from the grill. Let stand, covered with foil, for 10 minutes before cutting into diagonal slices. Editor's Note: See page 155 for the nutritional profile of this recipe.
    Yield: 12 servings

PORK CHOPS AND RICE

4 loin pork chops
meat tenderizer
seasoned salt to taste
vegetable oil
1/2 cup rice

Season the pork chops with meat tenderizer and seasoned salt. Place enough vegetable oil in a skillet to cover the bottom. Heat until hot. Add the pork chops. Cook until browned. Add the rice and water to cover. Simmer, covered, for 20 minutes or until the water is absorbed.
    Yield: 4 servings

CAJUN PORK CHOPS

1 tablespoon paprika

1$\frac{1}{2}$ teaspoons garlic powder

1 teaspoon each onion powder and ground cumin

$\frac{1}{2}$ teaspoon each dried oregano, dried basil and celery salt

$\frac{1}{2}$ teaspoon filé powder (optional)

$\frac{1}{2}$ teaspoon each cayenne pepper, white pepper, black pepper and salt

$\frac{1}{8}$ teaspoon ground mace

6 (2$\frac{1}{2}$-pound) pork chops, fat trimmed

Mix the paprika, garlic powder, onion powder, cumin, oregano, basil, celery salt, filé powder, cayenne, white pepper, black pepper, salt and mace in a bowl. Rub about 1 teaspoon of the mixture into each pork chop. Let stand for 30 minutes. Preheat gas grill using medium setting. Grill the pork chops for 25 minutes or until cooked through, turning once. Editor's Note: See page 155 for the nutritional profile of this recipe.

Yield: 6 servings

SKILLET PORK CHOPS

4 loin pork chops

salt and pepper to taste

1 tablespoon vegetable oil

$\frac{1}{4}$ cup each chopped onion and green bell pepper

$\frac{1}{2}$ cup rice

1$\frac{1}{2}$ cups canned tomatoes

1 teaspoon salt

$\frac{1}{2}$ teaspoon sugar

$\frac{1}{2}$ teaspoon prepared mustard

Season the pork chops with salt and pepper. Heat the oil in a skillet. Add the pork chops. Cook until browned on both sides. Remove the pork chops. Sauté the onion and green pepper in the drippings in the skillet until tender. Stir in the rice, tomatoes, 1 teaspoon salt, sugar and mustard. Add the pork chops. Bring to a boil; reduce the heat. Simmer, covered, for 30 minutes or until the rice is tender and the pork chops are cooked through.

Yield: 4 servings

SZECHUAN-STYLE SPARERIBS

6 pounds pork spareribs
1 cup Szechuan sauce
1/4 cup dry sherry or apple juice
2 tablespoons minced gingerroot
1 teaspoon sesame oil

Arrange the spareribs in shallow glass dishes. Mix the Szechuan sauce, sherry, gingerroot and sesame oil in a bowl. Brush generously over the ribs. Chill, covered, for 1 to 2 hours. Remove the ribs from the marinade, reserving remaining marinade. Preheat gas grill using medium setting. Place a disposable foil pan in the center of the grill under the grids. Grill the ribs for 1 hour or until cooked through, turning occasionally and basting with the reserved marinade if desired. Editor's Note: See page 155 for the nutritional profile of this recipe.

Yield: 6 servings

COUNTRY RIBS WITH MUSTARD BARBECUE

2 cups prepared mustard
1 1/2 cups each catsup and white vinegar
1/4 cup vegetable oil
2 tablespoons Worcestershire sauce
3/4 to 1 cup sugar
6 cloves of garlic, minced
1 tablespoon crushed mustard seeds
1 teaspoon pepper
8 pounds country-style pork ribs

Combine the mustard, catsup, vinegar, oil, Worcestershire sauce, sugar, garlic, mustard seeds and pepper in a medium saucepan. Bring to a boil over high flame; reduce flame. Simmer for 10 minutes. Preheat gas grill using medium setting. Place a disposable foil pan in the center of the grill under the grids. Grill the ribs for 1 hour or until cooked through, turning several times and basting generously with the sauce. Serve with additional sauce.

Yield: 8 servings

DIJON HAM AND SWISS

3 cups flour
2 tablespoons sugar
$1/2$ teaspoon salt
2 packages fast-rising yeast
1 cup water
$1/4$ cup Dijon mustard
2 tablespoons margarine
1 cup flour
8 ounces cubed cooked ham
1 cup shredded Swiss cheese
$1/2$ cup chopped dill pickles
1 egg, beaten

Combine 3 cups flour, sugar, salt and yeast in a bowl and mix well. Set aside. Heat the water, Dijon mustard and margarine in a saucepan to 125 to 130 degrees, stirring occasionally. Add to the flour mixture and mix well. Add enough of the remaining 1 cup flour to make a soft dough.

Knead the dough on a floured surface for 4 minutes. Roll into a 12x14-inch rectangle on a greased baking sheet. Sprinkle the ham, cheese and dill pickle down the center $1/3$ of the dough length. Cut the dough from the filling to the edge at 1-inch intervals on each side; fold strips diagonally across the filling, sealing well. Cover and place over a large shallow pan half filled with boiling water. Let the dough rise for 15 minutes.

Preheat oven to 375 degrees. Brush the dough with the egg. Bake for 25 minutes. Serve warm.

Editor's Note: See page 155 for the nutritional profile of this recipe.

Yield: 4 servings

MICROWAVE HAM AND POTATOES

3 tablespoons butter
$1/3$ cup chopped onion
2 tablespoons flour
1 teaspoon salt
$1/8$ teaspoon red pepper flakes
$2^1/2$ cups milk
$1/4$ teaspoon dry mustard
5 potatoes, peeled, thinly sliced
2 cups cubed cooked ham

Mix the butter and onion in a 2-quart microwave-safe dish. Microwave, covered, on High for 3 to 5 minutes or until the onion is translucent.

Add the flour, salt and red pepper flakes to the onion mixture, stirring until smooth. Stir in the milk. Microwave on High for 8 to 12 minutes or until smooth and slightly thickened, stirring every 3 minutes. Stir in the mustard.

Place half the potatoes in the onion mixture in the dish. Sprinkle with the ham. Layer the remaining potatoes over the ham, pressing into the onion mixture.

Microwave, covered, on High for 10 minutes; stir to mix. Microwave, covered, for 9 to 13 minutes longer or until the potatoes are tender.

Editor's Note: See page 155 for the nutritional profile of this recipe.

Yield: 6 servings

GRILLED HAM

1 (3-pound) canned ham, cut into $1/2$-inch slices
1 (6-ounce) can frozen orange juice concentrate, thawed
$1/4$ cup brown sugar
$1/2$ teaspoon allspice
1 teaspoon Worcestershire sauce
1 cup ginger ale or clear soda

Place the ham in a shallow dish. Mix the orange juice concentrate, brown sugar, allspice, Worcestershire sauce and ginger ale in a bowl. Spoon over the ham. Marinate, covered, in the refrigerator for several hours to overnight. Preheat gas grill using medium setting. Remove the ham from the marinade, reserving remaining marinade. Grill the ham until lightly browned and heated through, turning once and brushing occasionally with the reserved marinade. Editor's Note: See page 155 for the nutritional profile of this recipe.
  Yield: 8 servings

CRUNCHY HAM SANDWICHES

butter or margarine, softened
8 slices white bread
4 slices ham
4 slices American cheese
1 tomato, thinly sliced
prepared mustard to taste
2 eggs, lightly beaten
2 tablespoons milk
$1/8$ teaspoon onion salt, or to taste
$1 1/4$ cups crushed potato chips

Spread butter on 1 side of 4 slices of the bread. Layer 1 slice ham, 1 slice cheese and 1 to 2 tomato slices on each of the buttered bread slices. Spread mustard on the remaining bread and place bread on top of the sandwiches. Mix the eggs, milk and onion salt in a shallow dish. Dip each side of the sandwiches in the egg mixture, then in the potato chips, patting to push the potato chips into the bread. Place the sandwiches in a lightly greased skillet. Cook for 2 minutes per side or until browned and crisp.
  Yield: 4 servings

GRILLED ITALIAN SAUSAGE ON INDIVIDUAL PIZZAS

1 pound hot or mild Italian sausage
2 pita breads
olive oil or vegetable oil
$3/4$ cup prepared pizza sauce or spaghetti sauce
1 cup shredded mozzarella cheese

Preheat gas grill using medium setting. Grill the sausage for 20 to 30 minutes or until cooked through, turning occasionally. Cut the sausage into $1/2$-inch pieces. Cut the bread into halves horizontally to make 4 rounds. Brush the cut surfaces with olive oil. Grill the bread for 1 to 2 minutes per side or until lightly toasted. Spread the cut surfaces of the bread with 2 to 3 tablespoons of the pizza sauce; top with the grilled sausage and cheese. Place the pizzas in a large shallow baking pan. Grill, covered lightly with heavy-duty foil, for 3 to 5 minutes or until the cheese melts.

   Yield: 4 servings

CHICKEN CORDON BLEU

2 boneless chicken breasts, split into halves
salt and pepper to taste
2 slices cooked ham, cut into halves
2 slices Swiss cheese, cut into halves
$1/2$ cup milk
1 egg, beaten
$1/2$ cup flour
$3/4$ cup dry bread crumbs
$1/3$ cup butter

Flatten the chicken on waxed paper with a meat mallet. Season with salt and pepper. Top each chicken piece with ham and cheese. Roll each up as for a jelly roll. Dredge in the flour and dip in a mixture of the milk and egg. Coat well with the bread crumbs. Preheat oven to 375 degrees. Melt the butter in a heavy skillet. Add the chicken rolls. Cook until browned on both sides. Remove to a baking dish. Bake for 20 to 25 minutes or until the chicken is cooked through. Serve plain or with a favorite cheese sauce.

   Yield: 4 servings

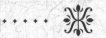 CHICKEN WITH CORN BREAD AND BOURBON PECAN STUFFING

1 medium onion, chopped
1 cup celery, chopped
$1/2$ cup julienned red bell pepper
$1/4$ cup butter
$1/2$ cup pecan halves
3 tablespoons bourbon
6 chicken breasts
salt and pepper to taste
30 prewashed spinach leaves
2 cups corn bread stuffing
6 smoked sausage links, cooked, drained

Preheat oven to 375 degrees. Cook the onion, celery and red pepper in the butter in a skillet until tender. Set aside. Heat the pecans in the bourbon in a small saucepan. Set aside.

Place the chicken between sheets of plastic wrap. Flatten each with a meat mallet. Season with salt and pepper. Top each piece with 5 spinach leaves. Spoon corn bread stuffing over the spinach; top with pecans. Cover with a sausage link. Roll each piece up as for a jelly roll. Cover each piece with foil.

Pour a small amount of water into a baking pan. Add the chicken rolls. Bake for 35 minutes or until the chicken is cooked through.

Yield: 6 servings

CHICKEN ROYALE

$1/2$ cup sour cream
1 tablespoon lemon juice
1 teaspoon Worcestershire sauce
1 teaspoon celery salt
$1/2$ teaspoon paprika
$1/2$ clove of garlic, minced
1 teaspoon salt
$1/8$ teaspoon pepper
3 chicken breast halves, skin removed
$1 1/4$ cups fine soft bread crumbs
$1/4$ cup melted butter or margarine

Combine the sour cream, lemon juice, Worcestershire sauce, celery salt, paprika, garlic, salt and pepper in a bowl and mix well. Coat the chicken with the mixture. Place in a shallow dish or pan. Marinate, covered, in the refrigerator overnight.

Preheat oven to 350 degrees. Coat the chicken with bread crumbs. Arrange in a single layer in a shallow baking pan. Spoon half the butter over the chicken. Bake for 45 minutes. Spoon the remaining butter over the chicken. Bake for 15 minutes or until the chicken is cooked through.

Yield: 3 servings

HONEY PINEAPPLE CHICKEN BREASTS

3/4 cup clover honey
1/2 cup pineapple preserves
2 tablespoons finely chopped gingerroot
2 tablespoons finely chopped mint
6 boneless chicken breast halves

Preheat gas grill using medium setting. Mix the honey, preserves, gingerroot and mint in a bowl. Grill the chicken for 25 minutes or until cooked through, turning occasionally and basting with the honey mixture. Serve with remaining honey mixture. Editor's Note: See page 155 for the nutritional profile of this recipe.

Yield: 6 servings

PEPPERCORN CHICKEN

2 pounds chicken pieces
2 cups dry white wine
2 tablespoons white Worcestershire sauce
3 tablespoons drained crushed green peppercorns
2 tablespoons minced parsley
2 cloves of garlic, minced

Arrange the chicken in a shallow glass dish. Mix the wine, Worcestershire sauce, peppercorns, parsley and garlic in a bowl. Pour over the chicken. Chill, covered, for 2 to 3 hours. Remove the chicken from the marinade, reserving the remaining marinade. Preheat gas grill using medium setting. Grill the chicken for 45 minutes or until cooked through, turning occasionally and brushing with the reserved marinade. Editor's Note: See page 155 for the nutritional profile of this recipe.

Yield: 6 servings.

CHICKEN LEGS WITH CHILI BARBECUE SAUCE

3 pounds chicken legs
Chili Barbecue Sauce

Preheat gas grill using medium setting. Grill the chicken for 1 hour or until cooked through, basting generously with Chili Barbecue Sauce every 10 to 15 minutes. Serve with remaining sauce.

Yield: 4 to 6 servings

CHILI BARBECUE SAUCE

$1^3/_4$ cups catsup
$^1/_2$ cup light molasses
$^1/_4$ cup chili sauce
2 tablespoons Dijon mustard
2 tablespoons cider vinegar
1 cup chopped onion
3 cloves of garlic, minced
3 tablespoons dark brown sugar

Combine the catsup, molasses, chili sauce, Dijon mustard, vinegar, onion, garlic and brown sugar in a medium saucepan. Bring to a boil over high flame; reduce flame. Simmer for 20 minutes.

CHICKEN TANDOORI

1 (2¹/2-pound) roasting chicken, cut into quarters
2 cups plain yogurt
3 cloves of garlic, minced
1 tablespoon paprika
2 teaspoons ground cinnamon
1¹/4 teaspoons ground cumin
1 teaspoon ground coriander
¹/2 teaspoon ground ginger
¹/2 teaspoon ground cloves
¹/2 teaspoon ground nutmeg
¹/2 teaspoon ground cardamom
¹/2 teaspoon ground turmeric
¹/2 teaspoon salt
¹/2 teaspoon white pepper

Arrange the chicken in a shallow glass dish. Combine the yogurt, garlic, paprika, cinnamon, cumin, coriander, ginger, cloves, nutmeg, cardamom, turmeric, salt and white pepper in a bowl and mix well. Pour over the chicken.

Marinate the chicken, covered, in the refrigerator for 8 hours to overnight, turning several times. Remove the chicken from the marinade, discarding the remaining marinade.

Preheat gas grill using medium setting. Place the chicken skin side up on the grill. Grill for 1 hour or until the chicken is cooked through, turning occasionally. Serve with lemon wedges.

Editor's Note: See page 155 for the nutritional profile of this recipe.

Yield: 4 servings

ORANGE-SCENTED CHICKEN

1 (3-pound) chicken
1 medium orange, cut into quarters
vegetable oil
$1/4$ teaspoon dried rosemary
$1/4$ teaspoon dried thyme
paprika to taste

Stuff the chicken cavity with the orange pieces. Truss the chicken; cut off and discard the wing tips. Brush the chicken lightly with oil; sprinkle with the rosemary, thyme and paprika. Preheat gas grill using medium setting. Place a disposable foil pan in the center of the grill under the grids. Grill the chicken for 1 hour or until cooked through. Remove from the grill. Let stand, covered loosely with foil, for 10 minutes before carving. Discard the orange pieces. Editor's Note: See page 155 for the nutritional profile of this recipe.

Yield: 4 servings

CHIP AND DIP CHICKEN

1 ($2^1/2$- to 3-pound) fryer, cut up
salt and pepper to taste
1 (8-ounce) package onion dip
$1^1/2$ cups crushed potato chips

Preheat oven to 350 degrees. Season the chicken with salt and pepper. Coat each piece with onion dip and then with potato chip crumbs. Place on a foil-lined baking sheet. Bake for 1 hour.

Yield: 4 servings

APRICOT GINGER CHICKEN

1/2 cup apricot preserves
1/4 cup cider vinegar
2 tablespoons vegetable oil
1 1/2 teaspoons ground ginger
1 (2 1/2- to 3-pound) fryer, cut into halves
salt and pepper to taste

Preheat gas grill using medium setting. Mix the apricot preserves, vinegar, oil and ginger in a bowl. Season the chicken with salt and pepper. Place the chicken skin side up on the grill. Grill for 30 to 40 minutes, turning every 10 minutes. Grill for 20 minutes longer or until cooked through, brushing every 5 minutes with the ginger mixture. Editor's Note: See page 155 for the nutritional profile of this recipe.

Yield: 4 servings

ORANGE-GLAZED CORNISH HENS

1 (6-ounce) package wild rice mix
1/4 cup orange marmalade
1/4 cup prepared mustard
2 tablespoons brown sugar
1/2 cup orange juice
salt and pepper to taste
6 Cornish game hens
softened margarine

Preheat oven to 350 degrees. Prepare the rice using the package directions. Mix the marmalade, mustard, brown sugar and orange juice in a bowl and set aside. Salt and pepper the hen cavities. Rub each hen with margarine. Fill each cavity with 1/2 cup of the rice mixture. Place the hens on a rack in a roasting pan. Bake for 45 minutes or until the hens are cooked through, basting every 15 minutes with the marmalade mixture. Editor's Note: See page 155 for the nutritional profile of this recipe.

Yield: 6 servings

GRILLED TURKEY WITH ITALIAN-STYLE RICE STUFFING

2 cups long grain rice
2 tablespoons vegetable oil
5 cups water
2 tablespoons instant chicken bouillon
12 ounces hot or mild Italian sausage
3/4 cup chopped onion
2 cloves of garlic, minced
1 (4-ounce) can sliced mushrooms, drained
2 teaspoons crushed fennel seeds
1/2 cup grated Parmesan cheese
salt and pepper to taste
1 (12- to 14-pound) fresh or thawed frozen turkey
paprika to taste

Sauté the rice in 2 tablespoons oil in a large skillet over medium flame until golden brown. Combine the rice, water and instant bouillon in a large saucepan. Cook using the package directions, omitting the salt.

Brown the sausage in a large skillet over medium flame; drain well, reserving 1 tablespoon drippings. Remove the sausage and cut into 1/2-inch pieces.

Sauté the onion, garlic, mushrooms and fennel seeds in the reserved drippings for 5 minutes or until the onion is tender. Stir the sausage, onion mixture and cheese into the cooked rice. Season with salt and pepper.

Preheat gas grill using medium setting. Spoon the rice mixture into the turkey cavity. Truss the turkey, securing with metal skewers or kitchen string. Brush the turkey lightly with additional oil; sprinkle with paprika.

Place a disposable foil pan in the center of the grill under the grids. Place the turkey breast side up on the grill. Grill for 13 to 15 minutes per pound or until a meat thermometer registers 180 degrees. Remove the turkey from the grill. Let stand, loosely covered with foil, for 10 minutes before carving.

Editor's Note: See page 155 for the nutritional profile of this recipe.
Yield: 14 servings

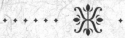

GRILLED STUFFED TURKEY

¹/4 cup butter, cut into slices
whole thyme leaves
1 (12- to 14-pound) fresh or thawed frozen turkey
sliced carrots, celery and onions

Slip the butter and thyme under the skin of the turkey. Place the sliced vegetables in the turkey cavity and truss the turkey. Preheat double burner gas grill on high setting for 10 minutes. Place a pan of water directly on the lava rocks on 1 side of the grill. Turn off the side with the water under it; adjust the other side to medium-high. Place the turkey on a roasting rack in a baking pan. Set on the grid over the pan of water; this side is not turned on. Grill for 17 minutes per pound or until the turkey is cooked through.

Yield: 12 to 14 servings

BRAISED TURKEY SHANKS

¹/4 cup olive oil
2 pounds turkey thighs, cut across the bone
2 tablespoons finely chopped fresh gingerroot
1 cup chopped onion
2 tablespoons chopped garlic
1 teaspoon each black pepper and salt
3 cups chicken stock or water
2 teaspoons chopped cilantro
¹/2 cup each chopped yellow bell pepper and orange bell pepper
1 tomato, chopped
1 cup chopped spinach

Preheat a large stockpot over medium heat. Add the olive oil and turkey. Braise for 10 minutes. Add the gingerroot, onion, garlic, pepper and salt. Add the chicken stock. Simmer, covered, for 30 minutes. Add the cilantro, bell peppers, tomato and spinach. Simmer for 10 minutes longer. Serve with your favorite vegetables and Sweet Potato Dumplings (page 127). Editor's Note: See page 155 for the nutritional profile of this recipe.

Yield: 6 servings

TURKEY WITH TOMATILLO SALSA

1¹/₂ pounds boneless turkey breast slices
Tomatillo Salsa

Preheat gas grill using medium setting. Grill the turkey for 25 minutes or until cooked through, turning occasionally and basting with Tomatillo Salsa. Serve with remaining salsa.

Yield: 6 servings

TOMATILLO SALSA

¹/₂ cup chopped onion
¹/₂ cup chopped green bell pepper
1 clove of garlic, minced
1 fresh or canned jalapeño, finely chopped
2 tablespoons vegetable oil
1 pound tomatillos, husks removed, coarsely chopped
¹/₄ cup water
salt and white pepper to taste

Sauté the onion, green pepper, garlic and jalapeño in the oil in a small saucepan for 5 minutes or until tender. Add the tomatillos and water. Bring to a boil over high flame; reduce flame. Simmer for 5 minutes or until the tomatillos are tender. Season with salt and pepper.

BREADED TURKEY CUTLETS

1 cup unseasoned dry bread crumbs
$1/2$ teaspoon dried basil
$1/2$ teaspoon dried thyme
$1/4$ teaspoon dried oregano
$1/4$ teaspoon garlic powder
$1/4$ teaspoon salt
$1/4$ teaspoon pepper
$1^1/2$ pounds turkey breast, cut into $1/2$-inch slices
1 egg, lightly beaten
3 tablespoons vegetable oil

Mix the bread crumbs, basil, thyme, oregano, garlic powder, salt and pepper in a shallow bowl or pan. Dip the turkey slices into the egg, then coat generously with the crumb mixture. Heat the oil in a large skillet over medium flame. Add the turkey. Cook for 10 minutes or until cooked through, turning frequently.

Yield: 6 servings

HERB AND SPICE RUB

3 cloves of garlic, minced
2 tablespoons dry mustard
2 tablespoons paprika
2 tablespoons pepper
1 tablespoon dried marjoram
1 tablespoon dried thyme
2 tablespoons Worcestershire sauce
2 tablespoons vegetable oil

Combine the garlic, mustard, paprika, pepper, marjoram, thyme, Worcestershire sauce and oil in a food processor container or blender container. Process until smooth. Rub onto both sides of steaks or chops. Let stand for 1 to 2 hours before grilling.

Yield: $1/3$ cup

🔥 CINNAMON APRICOT GLAZE

$1/2$ cup each apricot nectar and catsup
2 tablespoons each dark molasses and white wine vinegar
$1/2$ teaspoon each ground cinnamon and celery seeds
2 tablespoons vegetable oil

Mix the apricot nectar, catsup, molasses, vinegar, cinnamon and celery seeds in a medium bowl. Add the oil gradually, whisking constantly until blended. Use as a glaze to brush on chicken or ribs during grilling.
   Yield: 1 1/4 cups

🔥 TARRAGON MUSTARD SAUCE

$1/2$ cup spicy brown mustard
2 teaspoons dried tarragon
$1/4$ teaspoon pepper
1 tablespoon each balsamic vinegar and white wine vinegar
$1/2$ cup vegetable oil

Mix the mustard, tarragon, pepper, balsamic vinegar and wine vinegar in a medium bowl. Add the oil gradually, whisking constantly until blended. Use as a sauce to brush on poultry, pork or fish during grilling.
   Yield: 1 cup

🔥 SPICY JAMAICAN JERK

$1/2$ cup Montego Jerk Jamaican Pepper Sauce
$1/4$ cup each lime juice and water
2 tablespoons extra-virgin olive oil
$1/4$ teaspoon allspice
1 clove of garlic, minced

Mix the pepper sauce, lime juice, water, olive oil, allspice and garlic in a bowl. Pour over chicken, pork, lamb or beef. Marinate in the refrigerator for 2 hours. Brush the meat with reserved marinade during grilling.
   Yield: 1 cup

CHAPTER FOUR

SEAFOOD AND MEATLESS ENTREES

CATFISH WITH PINE NUTS AND MANGO CHUTNEY

1 tablespoon seasoning salt
1/2 tablespoon granulated garlic
1 teaspoon each chopped basil and oregano
pepper to taste
1/2 cup olive oil
2 tablespoons soy sauce
1 teaspoon chopped shallots
2 (4-ounce) catfish fillets
2 tablespoons olive oil
1/2 cup white wine
2 tablespoons butter
2 tablespoons toasted pine nuts
salt to taste

Mix the seasoning salt, garlic, basil, oregano and pepper in a small bowl. Mix 1/2 cup olive oil, soy sauce and shallots in a shallow dish. Rub the catfish with the spice mixture and place in the soy sauce mixture. Marinate for several minutes. Remove the catfish from the marinade, discarding remaining marinade. Heat 2 tablespoons olive oil in a medium skillet. Add the catfish. Cook until browned on both sides. Remove the catfish to a serving platter and keep warm. Add the wine to the skillet. Cook until somewhat reduced. Add the butter and swirl to mix. Add the pine nuts, salt and additional pepper. Spoon over the catfish. Serve with Mango Chutney.

Yield: 2 servings

MANGO CHUTNEY

2 ripe mangos, chopped
1 cucumber, peeled, seeded, chopped
2 green onions, finely chopped
1 tablespoon finely chopped cilantro
1 tablespoon brown sugar
juice of 11/2 limes

Mix the mangos, cucumber, green onions, cilantro, brown sugar and lime juice in a bowl.

 GRILLED YELLOWFIN GROUPER WITH BUTTER PECAN SAUCE

4 grouper fillets
seasoned flour
vegetable oil
Butter Pecan Sauce

Preheat gas grill using medium setting. Lightly dust the grouper with seasoned flour and brush with oil. Grill for 3 to 4 minutes per side or until the grouper flakes easily. Serve topped with Butter Pecan Sauce and garnished with chopped parsley.

Yield: 4 servings

Butter Pecan Sauce

3 tablespoons finely chopped shallots
$3/4$ cup dry white wine
1 tablespoon Champagne vinegar
3 tablespoons whipping cream
3 tablespoons rich chicken stock
3 tablespoons lemon juice
$1/2$ cup cold butter
salt and pepper to taste
$1/3$ cup honey roasted pecans

Combine the shallots, wine, vinegar, whipping cream, chicken stock and lemon juice in a medium saucepan. Bring to a vigorous boil. Cook until reduced by about $2/3$. Reduce heat to medium flame. Add the butter 1 tablespoon at a time, whisking until melted. Strain the sauce through a sieve. Add salt, pepper and pecans and mix well.

AMBERJACK PARMESAN

$1/4$ cup fresh bread crumbs
$1/4$ cup grated Parmesan cheese
$1/4$ teaspoon curry powder
$1/4$ teaspoon lemon pepper
$1/4$ teaspoon paprika
$1/4$ teaspoon oregano
12 ounces amberjack fillets
$2^1/2$ tablespoons melted margarine

Preheat oven to 400 degrees. Mix the bread crumbs, cheese, curry powder, lemon pepper, paprika and oregano in a bowl. Arrange the fish in a greased casserole. Spread the cheese mixture over the fish. Pour the margarine over the top. Bake for 15 minutes or until the fish flakes easily.
   Yield: 2 servings

ORANGE ROUGHY IN LAYERS

2 pounds orange roughy fillets
vegetable oil
6 thin slices tomato
6 thin slices green bell pepper
3 green onions, cut lengthwise into halves
6 sprigs of parsley
pepper to taste

Preheat gas grill using medium setting. Brush the orange roughy lightly with oil. Place half the orange roughy in a hinged grill basket. Top with the tomato, green pepper, green onions, parsley and remaining orange roughy. Grill for 7 to 10 minutes per side or until the orange roughy flakes easily. Arrange the fish on a serving plate, discarding the parsley. Editor's Note: See page 155 for the nutritional profile of this recipe.
   Yield: 6 servings

SALMON LOAF WITH CUCUMBER SAUCE

1 (16-ounce) can salmon, drained, flaked
$1/2$ cup dry bread crumbs
$1/2$ cup mayonnaise
$1/2$ cup chopped onion
$1/4$ cup chopped celery
$1/4$ cup chopped green bell pepper
1 egg, beaten
1 teaspoon salt
Cucumber Sauce

Preheat oven to 350 degrees. Combine the salmon, bread crumbs, mayonnaise, onion, celery, green pepper, egg and salt in a bowl and mix lightly. Shape into a loaf in a shallow baking dish. Bake for 40 minutes. Serve with Cucumber Sauce.

Yield: 4 to 6 servings

CUCUMBER SAUCE

$1/2$ cup mayonnaise
$1/2$ cup sour cream
$1/2$ cup finely chopped cucumber
2 tablespoons chopped onion
$1/2$ teaspoon dillweed

Combine the mayonnaise, sour cream, cucumber, onion and dillweed in a bowl and mix well.

GRILLED SEA BASS

1 teaspoon each dried basil, thyme, oregano and black pepper
2 teaspoons each seasoning salt and chicken-flavor base
1/4 cup each white wine and soy sauce
1 cup olive oil
3 tablespoons lime juice
1 cup thinly sliced onions
2 tablespoons chopped cilantro
3 cloves of garlic, minced
1 serrano pepper, seeded, chopped
1 tablespoon black pepper
4 (5- to 6-ounce) sea bass fillets

Mix the basil, thyme, oregano, 1 teaspoon black pepper, seasoning salt and chicken base in a small bowl. Mix next 9 ingredients in a medium bowl. Rub the sea bass with the herb mixture and place in a shallow glass dish or stainless steel pan. Pour the wine mixture over the sea bass. Marinate, covered, in the refrigerator for 2 hours to overnight. Preheat gas grill using medium setting. Remove the sea bass from the marinade, discarding the remaining marinade. Grill the sea bass until browned and tender.
    Yield: 4 servings

LEMON SNAPPER

3 pounds snapper fillets
1/2 cup olive oil
1/4 cup lemon juice
1 teaspoon oregano
salt and pepper to taste
1/2 teaspoon garlic powder (optional)

Preheat oven to 350 to 375 degrees. Place the snapper in a shallow baking pan. Mix the olive oil, lemon juice, oregano, salt, pepper and garlic powder in a bowl. Pour enough of the mixture over the snapper to cover the bottom of the pan, reserving the remaining mixture. Bake for 10 minutes or until the snapper flakes easily. Remove from the oven. Pour the remaining lemon juice mixture over the fish. Serve hot.
Editor's Note: See page 155 for the nutritional profile of this recipe.
    Yield: 6 servings

GREEK-STYLE SNAPPER

1 large tomato, sliced
1 medium onion, sliced
4 (8-ounce) snapper fillets
juice of 1 lemon
1 tablespoon oregano
salt and white pepper to taste
minced garlic to taste
¼ cup melted butter
½ cup olive oil

Preheat oven to 350 degrees. Arrange the tomato and onion slices in a large baking dish. Top with the snapper. Sprinkle a small amount of lemon juice over the snapper. Season with the oregano, salt, white pepper and garlic. Pour the butter over the snapper. Add enough water to almost cover the snapper. Bake, covered, for 15 minutes. Remove the snapper to a serving plate. Mix the olive oil, remaining lemon juice and additional salt and white pepper in a bowl. Spoon over the snapper.

Yield: 4 servings

WHOLE RED SNAPPER SAN FRANCISCO

2 cups packed chopped fresh spinach
1½ cups sourdough bread crumbs
1 cup chopped tomato
6 slices bacon, crisp-cooked, crumbled
salt and pepper to taste
2 (1½-pound) whole red snapper, dressed
vegetable oil

Preheat gas grill using medium setting. Mix the spinach, bread crumbs, tomato, bacon, salt and pepper in a bowl. Spoon into the snapper, securing edges with metal skewers. Brush lightly with oil. Grill for 20 to 25 minutes or until the snapper is tender and flakes easily. Editor's Note: See page 155 for the nutritional profile of this recipe.

Yield: 6 servings

SOLE MILANESE

8 sole fillets
2 tablespoons vermouth
6 tablespoons olive oil
1 bay leaf
seasoned flour
2 eggs, lightly beaten
dry bread crumbs
olive oil for frying
6 tablespoons butter
1 clove of garlic, crushed
2 tablespoons chopped parsley
2 tablespoons drained capers
1 teaspoon chopped fresh oregano
juice of 1 lemon
salt and pepper to taste

Remove the skin from the fillets with a sharp knife; remove any small bones. Place the sole in a large shallow dish.

Mix the vermouth, 6 tablespoons olive oil and bay leaf in a small saucepan. Heat gently. Cool completely before pouring over the sole. Marinate the sole, covered, in the refrigerator for 1 hour, turning occasionally.

Remove the sole from the marinade, discarding the remaining marinade. Dredge the sole in seasoned flour, then dip in the eggs. Dip the sole in the bread crumbs, pressing the crumbs on firmly.

Heat a small amount of olive oil in a large skillet. Add the sole. Cook for 3 minutes per side or until golden brown. Remove and drain on paper towels. Arrange the sole on serving plates and keep warm.

Discard the olive oil from the skillet; wipe the skillet clean with paper towels. Add the butter and garlic to the skillet. Cook until heated through. Add the parsley, capers, oregano, lemon juice, salt and pepper and mix well. Spoon over the sole. Garnish with lemon wedges and additional parsley.

Yield: 8 servings

SWORDFISH STEAKS WITH BLENDER BEARNAISE SAUCE

4 (1-inch-thick) swordfish steaks
vegetable oil
Blender Béarnaise Sauce

Preheat gas grill using medium setting. Brush the swordfish lightly with oil. Grill for 5 to 10 minutes per side or until the swordfish is tender and flakes easily. Serve Blender Béarnaise Sauce over the swordfish.
Yield: 4 servings

BLENDER BEARNAISE SAUCE

$^1/_4$ cup tarragon vinegar
1 tablespoon lemon juice
1 tablespoon finely chopped shallots or onion
1 teaspoon dried tarragon
$^1/_4$ teaspoon dried chervil
3 egg yolks
$^1/_4$ teaspoon salt
1 cup melted margarine or butter

Combine the vinegar, lemon juice, shallots, tarragon and chervil in a small saucepan. Bring to a boil over medium-high flame; reduce flame. Simmer until reduced to 2 tablespoons, stirring constantly. Add the egg yolks and salt. Cook over very low heat until the mixture registers 160 degrees on a candy thermometer, stirring constantly. Cool quickly. Process in a blender at high speed until of the desired consistency, adding the melted margarine in a slow steady stream.

SEARED SESAME-GLAZED AHI TUNA STEAKS

1 cup light soy sauce
1 1/2 cups sesame oil
1 cup honey
3 tablespoons brown sugar
3 tablespoons roasted sesame seeds
10 (8-ounce) ahi tuna steaks

Combine the soy sauce, sesame oil, honey, brown sugar and sesame seeds in a small bowl and whisk until mixed. Add the tuna steaks. Marinate for 15 minutes. Remove the tuna from the marinade, reserving the remaining marinade. Heat a cast-iron skillet over medium heat for 5 minutes. Add the tuna. Cook for 2 to 4 minutes per side or until seared. Serve with lemon wedges and the reserved marinade for dipping. Editor's Note: See page 155 for the nutritional profile of this recipe.

Yield: 10 servings

TOASTED TUNA BUNS

1 (6-ounce) can flaked tuna, drained
2 tablespoons finely chopped onion
2 tablespoons chopped sweet pickle
2 tablespoons mayonnaise
4 hamburger buns
8 slices American cheese

Preheat broiler. Mix the tuna, onion, pickle and mayonnaise in a small bowl. Split the buns apart and spread each cut side with the tuna mixture. Top each with 1 slice cheese. Broil until the cheese is melted.

Yield: 8 servings

🔥 FISH FILLETS WITH CAPERS AND DILL

2 pounds fish fillets
1/3 cup finely chopped red bell pepper
1/4 cup finely chopped dill
2 tablespoons lemon juice
2 tablespoons drained capers

Preheat gas grill using medium setting. Place the fish on a large sheet of lightly greased heavy-duty foil. Top with the red pepper, dill, lemon juice and capers. Wrap the fish tightly in the foil. Grill for 15 to 20 minutes or until the fish is tender and flakes easily with a fork. Remove from the foil to serve. Editor's Note: See page 155 for the nutritional profile of this recipe.

   Yield: 6 servings

🔥 SEA SCALLOP KABOBS WITH MELON

1/3 cup vegetable oil
2 tablespoons lime juice
1 teaspoon poppy seeds
1 pound sea scallops
18 (1-inch) pieces cantaloupe or honeydew melon
6 thin slices smoked ham, cut into 1-inch strips

Preheat gas grill using medium setting. Mix the oil, lime juice and poppy seeds in a small bowl. Alternate the scallops and melon on skewers, threading the ham between in an S shape. Brush the kabobs with the lime juice mixture. Grill for 2 to 3 minutes per side or until the scallops are tender. Editor's Note: See page 155 for the nutritional profile of this recipe.

   Yield: 6 servings.

CRAB CAKES

1 pound lump crab meat
3 scallions
1 teaspoon butter
2/3 cup finely chopped onion
1/2 cup mayonnaise
1 egg, lightly beaten
1 teaspoon Worcestershire sauce
salt and cayenne pepper to taste
1 cup fine bread crumbs
3 tablespoons vegetable oil

Preheat oven to 350 degrees. Sift through the crab meat to remove any pieces of shell; set aside. Finely chop the green parts of the scallions, reserving the tops for a garnish.

Heat the butter in a small saucepan. Add the onion. Sauté over medium heat until tender. Cool slightly.

Combine the onion, mayonnaise, chopped scallions, egg and Worcestershire sauce in a bowl and mix well. Fold in the crab meat, trying to avoid breaking the larger pieces. Season with salt and cayenne. Add enough of the bread crumbs to hold the mixture together. Shape into 8 cakes.

Heat the oil in a large skillet. Add the crab cakes. Cook over high heat until browned on both sides. Remove to a baking dish with a slotted spatula.

Bake for 10 minutes or until heated through. Garnish with the reserved scallion tops. Serve with Rémoulade Sauce (page 101).

Editor's Note: See page 155 for the nutritional profile of this recipe.
Yield: 6 servings

REMOULADE SAUCE

2 cups mayonnaise
juice of 1 lemon
1 teaspoon Dijon mustard
1/2 teaspoon Worcestershire sauce
1/2 pickle
1 teaspoon drained capers
1 small shallot, peeled
1 clove of garlic
1/2 red bell pepper, seeded, coarsely chopped
4 sprigs of cilantro
4 sprigs of parsley
1 tablespoon Thai fish sauce
salt and freshly ground pepper

Combine the mayonnaise, lemon juice, Dijon mustard and Worcestershire sauce in a large bowl and mix well.

Combine the pickle, capers, shallot, garlic, red pepper, cilantro, parsley and fish sauce in a food processor container. Process until finely chopped.

Add the pickle mixture to the mayonnaise mixture and mix well. Season with salt and pepper. Serve with Crab Cakes (page 100).

Editor's Note: See page 155 for the nutritional profile of this recipe.

Yield: 6 servings

SESAME LIME LOBSTER TAILS

2 (1-pound) lobster tails, shells removed
Sesame Lime Butter
pepper to taste

Preheat gas grill using medium setting. Brush the lobsters with some of the Sesame Lime Butter; sprinkle with pepper. Grill for 10 to 15 minutes or until the lobster meat is opaque, turning and basting with Sesame Lime Butter occasionally. Serve with the remaining butter.

Yield: 2 servings

SESAME LIME BUTTER

1/2 cup butter or margarine
2 teaspoons toasted sesame seeds
1 teaspoon grated lime peel

Melt the butter in a small saucepan. Combine with the sesame seeds and lime peel in a small bowl and mix well.

BARBECUED SHRIMP

1^1/$_2$ teaspoons black pepper
1^1/$_2$ teaspoons red pepper flakes
1^1/$_2$ teaspoons white pepper
2 teaspoons salt
1^1/$_2$ teaspoons thyme
2 teaspoons minced garlic
1 teaspoon Worcestershire sauce
2 tablespoons butter
1^1/$_2$ pounds shrimp, peeled, deveined
^{1}/$_2$ cup shrimp stock
chopped green onions
^{1}/$_2$ cup warm beer

Combine the black pepper, red pepper flakes, white pepper, salt, thyme, garlic, Worcestershire sauce and butter in a skillet. Sauté until the mixture darkens; reduce flame.

Add the shrimp to the spice mixture. Sauté for 1^1/$_2$ minutes. Add half the shrimp stock. Cook for 1^1/$_2$ minutes. Turn the shrimp.

Add the remaining shrimp stock and green onions. Increase the flame to high. Add the beer. Cook for 1 minute. Serve warm in the pan juices.

Garnish with boiled small new potatoes and toast slices.

Yield: 4 servings

SHRIMP BOATS

4 small loaves French bread
16 large shrimp, peeled, deveined
$1/4$ cup vegetable oil
1 clove of garlic, minced
$1/8$ teaspoon hot pepper sauce, or to taste
1 cup shredded lettuce
Guacamole

Preheat gas grill using medium setting. Cut a thin slice from the top of each bread loaf; hollow out the loaves, leaving a $1/2$-inch shell in each. Thread the shrimp onto metal skewers. Mix the oil, garlic and hot pepper sauce in a small bowl. Brush over the shrimp. Grill for 5 to 10 minutes or until the shrimp turn pink. Fill the loaves with lettuce and Guacamole. Top with the shrimp.

   Yield: 4 servings

GUACAMOLE

1 avocado, peeled, seeded, coarsely mashed
$1/2$ cup mayonnaise or mayonnaise-type salad dressing
$1/2$ cup chopped tomato
1 tablespoon sliced green onions
2 tablespoons minced cilantro or parsley
2 teaspoons lemon juice
$1/8$ teaspoon salt, or to taste

Combine the avocado, mayonnaise, tomato, green onions, cilantro, lemon juice and salt in a bowl and mix well.

SHRIMP AND CHICKEN SAUTE

6 tablespoons sliced almonds
1/4 cup butter
1 1/2 pounds chicken, cooked, cut into bite-size pieces
1/2 to 3/4 chopped green bell pepper
1 medium onion, julienned
20 small mushrooms
12 ounces fresh shrimp, peeled, deveined
3 tablespoons Worcestershire sauce
6 tablespoons dry sherry

Toast the almonds or sauté in a small amount of butter in a skillet. Set aside. Melt 1/4 cup butter in a heavy skillet. Add the chicken. Sauté for 2 minutes. Add the green pepper, onion and mushrooms. Sauté until the green pepper is tender. Add the shrimp. Sauté until the shrimp turn pink. Add the Worcestershire sauce, sherry and almonds. Serve with rice topped with pan drippings. Editor's Note: See page 155 for the nutritional profile of this recipe.
   Yield: 4 servings

SHRIMP CYPRESS INN

4 ounces sliced mushrooms
1 1/2 tablespoons each parsley and minced fresh garlic
1/2 teaspoon Creole seasoning
1/2 cup butter or margarine
1/2 teaspoon lemon juice
2 tablespoons white wine
1 pound medium to large shrimp, peeled, deveined
1 (4-ounce) package angel hair pasta, cooked, drained
3 cups mixed shredded Cheddar cheese and mozzarella cheese

Preheat oven to 350 degrees. Sauté the mushrooms, parsley, garlic and Creole seasoning in the butter in a skillet until the mushrooms are tender. Add the lemon juice, wine and shrimp. Cook until the shrimp are almost done. Layer the pasta in 4 individual casseroles. Cover with the shrimp mixture. Top with cheese. Bake for 15 to 20 minutes or until bubbly. Editor's Note: See page 156 for the nutritional profile of this recipe.
   Yield: 4 servings

ORANGE AND ONION MARINADE

1 cup orange juice
1/4 cup vegetable oil
2 tablespoons white wine vinegar
2 tablespoons dark brown sugar
1 envelope onion soup mix
1/4 teaspoon pepper

Combine the orange juice, oil, vinegar, brown sugar, soup mix and pepper in a medium saucepan. Bring to a boil over medium-high flame; reduce flame. Simmer for 5 minutes, stirring constantly. Let cool before using as a marinade for fish or poultry to be grilled. Marinate fish for 30 minutes, poultry for 1 to 2 hours.

Yield: 1 1/4 cups

SAUCY SALSA

1 cup chopped tomato
1/4 cup chopped green bell pepper
1/4 cup sliced green onions
1/4 cup chopped cucumber
2 tablespoons finely chopped cilantro
1 tablespoon lime juice
salt and pepper to taste
hot pepper sauce to taste
sour cream or sour half-and-half (optional)

Combine the tomato, green pepper, green onions, cucumber, cilantro and lime juice in a medium bowl and mix well. Season with salt, pepper and hot pepper sauce. Serve over grilled seafood, steak or poultry, topped with sour cream.

Yield: 1 3/4 cups

LIGHT FETTUCCINI ALFREDO

2 cloves of garlic, minced
1 tablespoon melted margarine
1 tablespoon flour
$1^1/_3$ cups skim milk
2 tablespoons light cream cheese, softened
$^1/_2$ cup grated Parmesan cheese
1 (10-ounce) package frozen chopped broccoli, cooked, drained
4 cups hot drained cooked fettuccini
pepper to taste
2 teaspoons chopped fresh parsley

Sauté the garlic in the margarine in a skillet over medium heat until tender. Stir in the flour. Add the milk gradually, stirring constantly with a whisk until smooth. Cook for 8 minutes or until thickened, stirring constantly.

Stir the cream cheese into the flour mixture. Cook for 2 minutes. Add the Parmesan cheese and broccoli and mix well. Cook until the cheese melts. Fold in the hot fettuccini and toss well. Top with pepper and parsley.

Editor's Note: See page 156 for the nutritional profile of this recipe.

Yield: 4 servings

HOT PASTA PRIMAVERA

8 ounces broccoli, cut into florets
4 medium carrots, sliced
8 ounces mushrooms, sliced
8 ounces fettuccini, cooked, drained
2 to 3 tablespoons olive oil or vegetable oil
2 to 3 tablespoons lemon juice
2 tablespoons minced cilantro
1 teaspoon dried tarragon
$1/8$ teaspoon salt
$1/4$ teaspoon pepper
$1/2$ cup grated Parmesan cheese

Preheat gas grill using medium setting. Combine the broccoli and carrots with 1 inch of water in a medium saucepan. Bring to a boil over high flame; reduce flame. Simmer, covered, for 5 minutes; drain well.

Combine the broccoli, carrots, mushrooms and fettuccini in a 9x13-inch baking pan. Mix the olive oil, lemon juice, cilantro, tarragon, salt and pepper in a bowl. Drizzle over the fettuccini mixture and toss.

Grill, covered with heavy-duty foil, for 30 minutes or until the vegetables are tender-crisp. Sprinkle with the cheese and toss lightly.

Editor's Note: See page 156 for the nutritional profile of this recipe.
Yield: 6 servings

EASY SPINACH LASAGNA

1 (15-ounce) jar spaghetti sauce
2 (6-ounce) cans tomato paste
1 tablespoon basil
$1/4$ teaspoon pepper
$1/2$ teaspoon each oregano and minced garlic
1 (10-ounce) package frozen chopped spinach, thawed, drained
2 eggs, beaten
16 ounces cottage cheese or ricotta cheese
$1/2$ cup each grated Parmesan cheese and Romano cheese
8 ounces lasagna noodles
8 ounces mozzarella cheese, shredded

Preheat oven to 350 degrees. Mix the spaghetti sauce, tomato paste, basil, pepper, oregano and garlic in a medium bowl.

Mix the spinach, eggs, cottage cheese, half the Parmesan cheese and half the Romano cheese in a large bowl.

Spread $1/3$ of the sauce mixture over the bottom of a 9x13-inch baking dish. Add layers of $1/3$ of the lasagna noodles and $1/3$ of the spinach mixture. Repeat all layers twice more.

Sprinkle with the mozzarella cheese, remaining $1/4$ cup Parmesan cheese and $1/4$ cup Romano cheese. Bake, covered with foil, for $1 1/4$ hours. Let stand for 10 minutes before serving.

Editor's Note: See page 156 for the nutritional profile of this recipe.

Yield: 8 servings

TRI-COLOR VEGGIE PASTA

1 medium onion, thinly sliced
1 tablespoon olive oil
1 clove of garlic, cut into slivers
2 small yellow bell peppers, thinly sliced
2 small red bell peppers, thinly sliced
2 small zucchini, julienned
2 small yellow squash, julienned
salt and pepper to taste
8 ounces mostaccioli or other tube-shape pasta
3 tablespoons unsalted butter
3 tablespoons flour
$1^1/_2$ teaspoons rosemary
$^1/_2$ teaspoon sage
1 bay leaf
$1^1/_2$ cups milk
$1^1/_2$ cups shredded fontina cheese or shredded mozzarella cheese

Preheat oven to 425 degrees. Cook the onion in the olive oil in a large skillet until translucent. Add the garlic, yellow peppers and red peppers. Cook for 5 minutes, stirring frequently. Add the zucchini and yellow squash. Cook for 5 minutes longer, stirring frequently. Season with salt and pepper. Remove from the heat. Cook the pasta using the package directions; drain well.

Melt the butter in a large saucepan. Add the flour, rosemary, sage and bay leaf. Cook for 2 minutes, stirring constantly. Add the milk gradually, stirring constantly with a wire whisk. Cook until the mixture is the consistency of whipping cream, stirring constantly. Remove from the heat.

Combine the pasta, milk mixture, vegetable mixture and 1 cup of the cheese in a bowl and mix well. Spoon into a buttered 3-quart baking dish. Top with the remaining $^1/_2$ cup cheese. Bake for 20 to 30 minutes or until the top is crusty and browned.

Editor's Note: See page 156 for the nutritional profile of this recipe.

Yield: 8 servings

VEGETABLE AND CHEESE PIE

1 tablespoon butter
1 tablespoon vegetable oil
3 small yellow squash, thinly sliced
1 green bell pepper, chopped
3 tomatoes, peeled, sliced
3 egg yolks
3 egg whites, stiffly beaten
2 cups shredded Swiss cheese or Jarlsberg cheese
4 ounces feta cheese, crumbled
salt and pepper to taste

Preheat oven to 400 degrees. Heat the butter and vegetable oil in a skillet. Add the squash. Sauté until golden brown. Add the green pepper. Sauté for 5 minutes. Cook the tomatoes in a saucepan over medium heat for 2 minutes, stirring frequently. Beat the egg yolks in a mixer bowl until thick and pale yellow. Fold in the egg whites.

Layer half the squash mixture, 1/3 of the Swiss cheese, half the feta cheese, salt, pepper, half the egg mixture, tomatoes, 1/3 of the Swiss cheese, remaining feta cheese, remaining squash mixture, remaining egg mixture and remaining Swiss cheese in a buttered 10-inch pie plate.

Bake for 25 to 30 minutes or until set and golden brown.

Editor's Note: See page 156 for the nutritional profile of this recipe.

Yield: 6 servings

EGGS IN A RING

1 egg
1 cup milk
$1/4$ cup vegetable oil
1 cup all-purpose flour
1 cup whole wheat flour
1 cup shredded Cheddar cheese
2 tablespoons sugar
1 tablespoon baking powder
$1/2$ teaspoon salt
1 (10-ounce) package frozen green peas
1 (10-ounce) can cream of chicken soup
3 hard-cooked eggs, sliced
6 to 8 pimento-stuffed olives, sliced
2 tablespoons chopped onion
$1/8$ teaspoon poultry seasoning

Preheat oven to 400 degrees. Beat 1 egg in a bowl. Add the milk and oil and mix well. Add the all-purpose flour, whole wheat flour, cheese, sugar, baking powder and salt, stirring just until moistened. The batter will be lumpy. Spoon into a greased 6-cup ring mold. Bake for 20 to 25 minutes or until golden brown. Unmold onto a serving plate.

Combine the peas and soup in a 2-quart saucepan. Cook over medium heat until heated through, stirring occasionally. Add the sliced eggs, olives, onion and poultry seasoning and mix gently. Simmer for 3 to 5 minutes. Spoon into the center of the baked ring.

Editor's Note: See page 156 for the nutritional profile of this recipe.

Yield: 8 servings

CHAPTER FIVE

VEGETABLES AND SIDE DISHES

ASPARAGUS AND MUSHROOM CASSEROLE

4 cups mushroom halves

1 cup chopped onion

$1/4$ cup butter

2 teaspoons flour

1 teaspoon instant chicken bouillon

$1/2$ teaspoon salt

pepper to taste

$1/2$ teaspoon nutmeg

1 cup milk

2 (10-ounce) packages frozen cut asparagus, cooked, drained

$1/4$ cup chopped pimentos

$1/2$ cup sliced water chestnuts

$1^{1}/2$ teaspoons lemon juice

$3/4$ cup soft bread crumbs

1 teaspoon melted butter

Preheat oven to 350 degrees. Sauté the mushrooms and onion in $1/4$ cup butter in a saucepan for 10 minutes or until tender. Remove the vegetables to a bowl.

Stir the flour, instant bouillon, salt, pepper and nutmeg into the pan drippings in the saucepan. Add the milk and mix well. Cook until bubbly, stirring constantly.

Stir in the mushroom mixture, asparagus, pimentos, water chestnuts and lemon juice. Spoon into a $1^{1}/2$-quart baking dish.

Sprinkle the bread crumbs over the vegetables. Drizzle with 1 teaspoon melted butter. Bake for 35 minutes.

Yield: 8 to 10 servings

❋ BATCH OF BEANS

1 (16-ounce) can lima beans, drained
1 (16-ounce) can red kidney beans, drained
1 (15-ounce) can Great Northern beans
$1/2$ cup chopped onion
$1/2$ cup chopped green bell pepper
3 cloves of garlic, minced
1 cup clover honey
3 tablespoons Dijon mustard
$1/2$ teaspoon ground ginger
$1/4$ teaspoon ground nutmeg
$1/4$ teaspoon salt
$1/4$ teaspoon pepper

Preheat gas grill using medium setting. Combine the lima beans, kidney beans, undrained Great Northern beans, onion, green pepper and garlic in a bowl and mix well. Stir in the honey, Dijon mustard, ginger, nutmeg, salt and pepper. Spoon into a 9x9-inch baking pan. Grill, covered with heavy-duty foil, for 30 minutes or until heated through, stirring occasionally.

Yield: 6 to 8 servings

❋ GRILLED GREEN BEANS

1 (16-ounce) can whole green beans, drained
1 small onion, sliced
2 tablespoons margarine
salt and pepper to taste

Preheat gas grill using medium setting. Layer the green beans, onion slices and margarine on a sheet of heavy-duty foil; season with salt and pepper. Fold and seal the edges of the foil. Grill for 30 minutes or until heated through.

Yield: 2 servings

GREEN BEANS MEDITERRANEAN

1 pound green beans, trimmed, broken into pieces
1 large tomato, coarsely chopped
$1/2$ cup chopped onion
2 to 3 cloves of garlic, minced
2 tablespoons olive oil or vegetable oil
2 tablespoons tomato juice
$1/2$ teaspoon dried oregano
$1/4$ teaspoon each dried basil, salt and pepper

Preheat gas grill using medium setting. Combine the green beans, tomato, onion and garlic in a bowl and mix well. Spoon into a 9x9-inch baking pan. Drizzle with the olive oil and tomato juice. Sprinkle with the oregano, basil, salt and pepper and toss gently. Grill, covered with heavy-duty foil, for 45 minutes or until the beans are tender. Editor's Note: See page 156 for the nutritional profile of this recipe.

Yield: 6 servings

BRAISED CABBAGE

4 slices bacon, cut into $1/2$-inch pieces
1 cup coarsely chopped onion
$1/2$ cup chopped green bell pepper
2 cloves of garlic, minced
$1/2$ teaspoon crushed fennel seeds
1 medium head cabbage, thinly sliced
$1/2$ cup each chicken broth and dry white wine
salt and pepper to taste

Fry the bacon in a large saucepan over medium flame until crisp. Remove the bacon to paper towels. Drain all but 1 tablespoon bacon drippings from the saucepan. Add the onion, green pepper, garlic and fennel seeds to the saucepan. Sauté over medium flame until tender. Stir in the cabbage, chicken broth and wine. Bring to a boil over high flame; reduce flame. Simmer, covered, for 7 minutes or until the cabbage is wilted. Cook, uncovered, for 10 minutes or until the cabbage is tender. Season with salt and pepper. Crumble the bacon and stir into the cabbage mixture.

Yield: 4 to 6 servings

STEAMED RED CABBAGE

4 cups shredded red cabbage
1/2 cup chopped apple
3/4 cup chopped onion
1/4 cup white wine vinegar
2 tablespoons dark brown sugar
1 teaspoon caraway seeds

Preheat gas grill using medium setting. Mix the cabbage, apple, onion, vinegar, brown sugar and caraway seeds in a bowl. Spoon into an 8x8-inch baking pan. Grill, covered with heavy-duty foil, for 30 minutes or until the cabbage is tender, stirring occasionally.

Yield: 4 to 6 servings

JOHN NELSON'S FAMOUS CABBAGE ROLLS

12 large cabbage leaves
3/4 cup quick-cooking rice
1 egg, beaten
1 (8-ounce) can tomato sauce
1/4 cup milk
1 teaspoon each brown sugar and lemon juice
3/4 teaspoon garlic salt
1/4 teaspoon pepper
1 teaspoon Worcestershire sauce
1 pound ground chuck
chopped onion to taste
1 (28-ounce) can tomatoes

Preheat a slow cooker. Wash the cabbage leaves and immerse in boiling water until wilted; drain well. Mix the next 11 ingredients in a bowl. Spoon evenly onto the cabbage leaves. Fold the sides and ends of the leaves over the ground chuck mixture, securing with wooden picks. Place the cabbage rolls in the slow cooker. Pour the undrained tomatoes over the cabbage rolls. Cook for 8 to 10 hours. For spicier cabbage rolls, add red kidney beans, chile pepper and shredded cheese to the ground chuck mixture.

Yield: 6 servings

BAKED CARROTS

1 pound carrots, peeled, cut into quarters
$\frac{1}{2}$ teaspoon salt
$\frac{1}{8}$ teaspoon pepper
2 tablespoons butter

Preheat oven to 325 degrees. Place the carrots in a buttered 1-quart casserole. Sprinkle with a mixture of the salt and pepper. Dot with the butter. Bake, covered, for $1\frac{1}{4}$ hours or until the carrots are tender. Editor's Note: See page 156 for the nutritional profile of this recipe.
   Yield: 4 servings

CORN CASSEROLE

1 (16-ounce) can whole kernel corn, drained
1 (17-ounce) can cream-style corn
2 eggs, beaten
1 small onion, chopped
$\frac{1}{2}$ cup water
1 cup Jiffy corn muffin mix
$\frac{1}{4}$ cup margarine, softened

Preheat oven to 350 degrees. Combine the whole kernel corn, cream-style corn, eggs, onion, water, muffin mix and margarine in a bowl and mix well. Spoon into a 2-quart baking dish. Bake for 1 hour.
   Yield: 4 to 6 servings

 EL PASO SWEET CORN

12 ears fresh corn in husks
1/2 cup melted margarine or butter
2 tablespoons minced cilantro or parsley
2 teaspoons chili powder
1/4 teaspoon ground cumin
1/4 teaspoon garlic powder
1/4 teaspoon hot pepper sauce

Preheat gas grill using medium setting. Soak the corn in lukewarm water for 15 minutes; drain well. Mix the margarine, cilantro, chili powder, cumin, garlic powder and hot pepper sauce in a bowl. Pull the husks away from the corn; brush each ear generously with the margarine mixture. Pull the husks back over the corn; wrap each ear tightly in heavy-duty foil. Grill for 30 minutes or until the corn is tender, turning occasionally.

Yield: 8 servings

EASY CORN PUDDING

1 (10-ounce) package frozen corn kernels
1 cup whipping cream
3 eggs
1 tablespoon sugar
salt and pepper to taste
1/2 cup butter or margarine, sliced

Preheat oven to 350 degrees. Combine the corn, whipping cream, eggs, sugar, salt and pepper in a blender container. Process until mixed. Spoon into a greased casserole. Dot with the butter. Bake for 50 to 60 minutes or until set.

Yield: 4 to 6 servings

 ## KENYA GREENS

4 ounces country-style bacon, cut into cubes
1 onion, julienned
1 serrano pepper, chopped
1 clove of garlic, minced
$1^1/2$ pounds kale, julienned
$^1/8$ teaspoon sugar, or to taste
1 cup chicken stock
salt and pepper to taste

Cook the bacon in a large skillet until crisp. Remove the bacon and reserve for garnish. Add the onion, serrano pepper and garlic to the skillet. Cook for 1 minute. Add the kale and sugar. Cook until the liquid is reduced, adding chicken stock as needed. Season with salt and pepper. Garnish with the reserved bacon and cooked whole okra.
    Yield: 6 servings

PICKLED BLACK-EYED PEAS WITH PEPPERS
(Texas Caviar)

3 cups drained cooked black-eyed peas
$^1/2$ each red, yellow and green bell pepper, seeded, thinly sliced
4 green onions, thinly sliced
1 tablespoon chopped fresh cilantro
2 cloves of garlic, minced
$^3/4$ cup olive oil
$^1/2$ cup balsamic vinegar
$^1/8$ teaspoon crushed red pepper, or to taste
salt to taste

Combine the peas, all the peppers, green onions, cilantro, garlic, olive oil, vinegar, crushed red pepper and salt in a bowl and mix well. Chill, covered, overnight. May instead be served as an appetizer or with salad greens.
    Yield: 4 to 6 servings

EASY ENGLISH PEA CASSEROLE

1 (17-ounce) can English peas
1 (8-ounce) jar Cheez Whiz
3 hard-cooked eggs, chopped
1 (3-ounce) can French-fried onions

Preheat oven to 350 degrees. Cook the peas in a saucepan until heated through; drain well. Add the Cheez Whiz. Cook over low flame until the Cheez Whiz is melted, stirring occasionally. Remove from the heat. Stir in the eggs and half the onions. Spoon into a greased 1-quart casserole. Top with the remaining onions. Bake at 350 degrees for 10 minutes.

Yield: 6 servings

 CHEDDAR HASH BROWNS

4 large Idaho potatoes, cut into $1/2$-inch cubes
1 medium onion, coarsely chopped
$1/2$ medium green bell pepper, coarsely chopped
$1/2$ medium red bell pepper, coarsely chopped
$1/2$ teaspoon paprika
$1/2$ teaspoon salt
$1/4$ teaspoon pepper
3 tablespoons margarine or butter
1 cup shredded Cheddar cheese

Preheat gas grill using medium setting. Arrange the potatoes, onion, green pepper and red pepper in a 9x9-inch baking pan. Sprinkle with paprika, salt and pepper and toss lightly. Dot with the margarine. Grill, covered, with heavy-duty foil, for 30 minutes or until the potatoes are tender. Remove the foil and sprinkle with the cheese. Grill, uncovered, for 3 to 5 minutes or until the cheese is melted.

Yield: 4 to 6 servings

CRUSTY BAKED POTATOES

6 medium potatoes, peeled
1/4 cup melted butter
1/2 cup fine bread crumbs
1 teaspoon salt

Preheat oven to 350 degrees. Rinse the potatoes and wipe dry. Cut each into halves. Roll the potatoes in the butter, then in a mixture of the bread crumbs and salt. Arrange in a single layer in a baking pan. Bake for 1 hour.
Yield: 4 servings

 GRILLED PARMESAN SPUDS

3/4 cup grated Parmesan cheese
1/4 cup flour
1 teaspoon cayenne pepper
1/2 teaspoon black pepper
1/4 teaspoon salt
2 potatoes, peeled, cut into halves lengthwise
1/2 cup margarine or butter

Mix the cheese, flour, cayenne pepper, black pepper and salt in a bowl. Dampen the potato halves in water. Place the potatoes in the cheese mixture, turning to coat. Place a cast-iron skillet on gas grill briquets. Melt the margarine in the skillet over low flame. Add the potatoes to the skillet. Grill at medium setting with the cover closed for 35 minutes or until the potatoes are tender, turning once.
Yield: 2 servings

BAKED RED POTATOES AND FENNEL

6 new red potatoes, sliced
2 medium onions, sliced
2 fennel bulbs, sliced
1/2 teaspoon crushed celery seeds
1/4 teaspoon crushed caraway seeds
1/2 teaspoon salt
1/2 teaspoon pepper
3 tablespoons margarine or butter

Preheat gas grill using medium setting. Arrange the potatoes, onions and fennel in a 9x9-inch baking pan. Sprinkle with the celery seeds, caraway seeds, salt and pepper and toss well. Dot with the margarine. Grill, covered with heavy-duty foil, for 30 to 40 minutes or until the potatoes are tender.

Yield: 4 servings

POTATO BAKE

6 potatoes
1 (10-ounce) can cream of chicken soup
1 (10-ounce) can cream of mushroom soup
1/2 cup shredded Cheddar cheese

Preheat oven to 350 degrees. Boil the potatoes in water to cover until tender; drain well. Slice the potatoes and place in a baking pan. Spoon the chicken soup and mushroom soup over the potatoes. Top with the cheese. Bake for 10 minutes or until bubbly.

Yield: 4 to 6 servings

OVEN FRENCH FRIES

4 medium potatoes
1 tablespoon vegetable oil

Preheat oven to 475 degrees. Peel the potatoes and cut into long $1/2$-inch-wide strips. Dry the strips thoroughly with paper towels. Combine the potatoes and oil in a bowl, tossing to coat. Arrange the potatoes in a single layer on a baking sheet. Bake for 35 minutes or until browned on all sides, turning occasionally. May broil for 1 to 2 minutes after baking for crispier fries. Editor's Note: See page 156 for the nutritional profile of this recipe.

Yield: 6 servings

SPINACH MADELINE

2 (10-ounce) packages frozen spinach
$1/4$ cup butter
2 tablespoons flour
2 tablespoons chopped onion
$1/2$ cup evaporated milk
$1/2$ teaspoon black pepper
$3/4$ teaspoon each celery salt and garlic salt
1 teaspoon Worcestershire sauce
1 (6-ounce) roll jalapeño cheese, cut into small pieces
bread crumbs
red pepper flakes to taste

Preheat oven to 350 degrees. Cook the spinach using the package directions; drain, reserving $1/2$ cup of the cooking liquid. Melt the butter in a skillet over low heat. Add the flour, stirring constantly until blended but not browned. Stir in the onion. Add the evaporated milk and reserved cooking liquid gradually, stirring constantly until thickened and smooth. Add the pepper, celery salt, garlic salt, Worcestershire sauce and cheese. Cook until the cheese is melted, stirring constantly. Remove from the heat. Add the spinach and mix well. Spoon into a casserole. Sprinkle with bread crumbs and red pepper flakes. Bake for 30 minutes or until the casserole is heated through and the bread crumbs are browned. Better if prepared 1 day ahead. Freezes well.

Yield: 4 to 6 servings

SQUASH SOUFFLE

1 pound squash, chopped
1 large onion, chopped
8 to 10 saltine crackers, crumbled
$1/4$ cup butter, softened
2 egg yolks
1 cup shredded Cheddar cheese
$1/2$ cup milk
salt and pepper to taste
2 egg whites, stiffly beaten

Preheat oven to 350 degrees. Cook the squash and onion in water to cover in a saucepan until tender; drain well. Mix the squash mixture, cracker crumbs, butter, egg yolks, cheese, milk, salt and pepper in a bowl. Fold in the egg whites. Spoon into a greased casserole. Bake for 25 to 30 minutes or until golden brown and set. Serve hot.

Yield: 6 servings

SPAGHETTI SQUASH WITH PARMESAN HERB

1 (3-pound) spaghetti squash, cut lengthwise into halves, seeded
$1/4$ cup margarine or butter
2 cloves of garlic, minced
1 tablespoon minced parsley
$1/4$ teaspoon each salt and pepper
$1/4$ cup grated Parmesan cheese

Preheat gas grill using medium setting. Place squash cut side up on grill; cover loosely with heavy-duty foil. Grill for 1 hour or until almost tender. Combine the margarine, garlic, parsley, salt and pepper in a small saucepan with a heatproof handle. Place on the grill with the squash. Cook for 5 minutes or until the margarine is melted. Remove the squash from the grill; fluff with a fork into strands. Drizzle the margarine mixture over the squash. Sprinkle with the cheese and toss to mix. Return the squash to the grill. Grill for 5 minutes longer.

Yield: 4 servings

SQUASH CROQUETTES

5 pounds squash, chopped
3 cups chopped celery
2 cups chopped bell peppers
2 cups chopped onions
8 eggs
1 cup shredded cheese
1 tablespoon chopped parsley
3 tablespoons chicken-flavor base
$1/2$ teaspoon whole basil
1 teaspoon white pepper
$1/8$ teaspoon salt, or to taste
bread crumbs
vegetable oil for deep-frying

Combine the squash, celery, bell peppers, onions, eggs, cheese, parsley, chicken base, basil, white pepper and salt in a skillet. Sauté until the vegetables are tender. Shape into balls; roll in bread crumbs. Place on a baking sheet or tray sprinkled with bread crumbs. Chill thoroughly. Deep-fry in small batches in 350-degree oil for 5 to 6 minutes or until golden brown.

Yield: 225 croquettes

SQUASH AND ONIONS

6 medium yellow squash, cut into $1/2$-inch slices
3 medium onions, cut into $1/2$-inch slices
$1/4$ teaspoon garlic salt
salt and pepper to taste
2 tablespoons butter

Preheat gas grill using medium setting. Arrange the squash and onion slices alternately in rows on a large sheet of heavy-duty foil. Sprinkle with garlic salt, salt and pepper. Dot with the butter. Fold the foil over and seal tightly. Grill for 45 minutes or until the vegetables are tender.

Yield: 6 servings

GRILL-BAKED SWEET POTATOES WITH APRICOT BUTTER

8 medium sweet potatoes
6 tablespoons butter or margarine, softened
2 tablespoons apricot preserves
1/4 teaspoon ground cinnamon
1/4 teaspoon ground nutmeg

Preheat gas grill using medium setting. Grill the sweet potatoes for 45 minutes or until soft when pressed. Beat the butter in a small mixer bowl until fluffy. Beat in the preserves, cinnamon and nutmeg. Open the tops of the sweet potatoes and fluff with a fork. Spoon the apricot butter into the sweet potatoes. Editor's Note: See page 156 for the nutritional profile of this recipe.

Yield: 8 servings

SWEET POTATO DUMPLINGS

2 cups chopped sweet potatoes
1 cup sugar
2 cups water
1/2 cup butter, softened
1 tablespoon vanilla extract
1/2 cup flour
1 egg
1 cup hot fruit juice

Preheat oven to 350 degrees. Combine the sweet potatoes, sugar and water in a saucepan. Cook for 15 minutes; drain well. Place the sweet potatoes in a large bowl. Whip in the butter, vanilla, flour and egg. Pour the hot juice into a shallow casserole sprayed with nonstick cooking spray. Drop the sweet potato mixture by tablespoonfuls into the hot juice. Bake for 25 minutes.

Yield: 6 to 8 servings

FRIED GREEN TOMATOES

$1/4$ cup flour
1 tablespoon sugar
$1^1/2$ teaspoons salt
$1/8$ teaspoon pepper
4 green tomatoes, cut into $1/2$-inch slices
1 cup buttermilk
$1/4$ cup cornmeal
3 tablespoons (about) vegetable oil

Mix the flour, sugar, salt and pepper in a shallow dish. Dredge the tomatoes in the flour mixture. Dip the tomatoes in the buttermilk, then dredge in the cornmeal. Heat the oil in a skillet. Add the tomatoes. Fry until browned on both sides, adding additional oil if needed.

Yield: 4 servings

GRILLED VEGETABLES

2 (10-ounce) packages frozen asparagus, broccoli or mixed vegetables
1 teaspoon salt
$1/4$ teaspoon pepper
2 tablespoons butter, softened

Preheat gas grill using medium setting. Place frozen blocks of vegetables in the center of squares of heavy-duty foil. Sprinkle with salt and pepper. Dot with butter. Seal the foil with a double fold. Grill for 25 to 30 minutes or until the vegetables are tender, turning carefully several times.

Yield: 6 servings

 MARINATED VEGETABLE MEDLEY

8 ounces fresh or thawed frozen whole okra, tops trimmed
1 (8-ounce) zucchini, cut lengthwise into wedges
1 (8-ounce) yellow squash, cut lengthwise into wedges
1 large onion, cut into 1/2-inch slices
2 medium red bell peppers, cut into halves, seeded
2 medium leeks, cut into halves, or 8 green onions
Dill and Caraway Marinade

Place all the vegetables in a sealable large plastic bag. Add Dill and Caraway Marinade and seal. Place the bag in a large bowl. Marinate for 2 to 4 hours, turning the bag occasionally. Preheat gas grill using medium setting. Remove the vegetables from the marinade, reserving the remaining marinade. Place the vegetables on the grill. Grill for 20 minutes or until browned, turning occasionally and basting with the reserved marinade.

Yield: 4 servings

DILL AND CARAWAY MARINADE

1 cup olive oil or vegetable oil
1/3 cup red wine vinegar
1 tablespoon white Worcestershire sauce
2 teaspoons Dijon mustard
2 cloves of garlic, minced
3/4 teaspoon dried dillweed
3/4 teaspoon crushed caraway seeds

Combine the olive oil, vinegar, Worcestershire sauce, Dijon mustard, garlic, dillweed and caraway seeds in a bowl and mix well.

ORIENTAL WILD RICE

1 (6-ounce) package mixed long grain and wild rice
$2\frac{1}{3}$ cups water
4 ounces snow peas
1 cup sliced mushrooms
$\frac{1}{4}$ cup sliced green onions
2 tablespoons sesame oil or melted margarine
2 cloves of garlic, minced
1 to 2 teaspoons finely chopped gingerroot
$\frac{1}{4}$ teaspoon each Chinese five-spice powder, salt and pepper

Preheat gas grill using medium setting. Cook the rice in the water using the package directions; discard the seasoning packet or reserve for another use.

Combine the rice, snow peas, mushrooms and green onions in a large bowl and mix well. Spoon into a 9x9-inch baking pan.

Combine the sesame oil, garlic, gingerroot, five-spice powder, salt and pepper in a medium bowl and mix well. Drizzle over the rice mixture and toss lightly. Grill, covered with heavy-duty foil, for 20 minutes or until the snow peas are tender-crisp.

Yield: 4 to 6 servings

POLYNESIAN RICE

4 cups hot cooked rice
2 tablespoons butter or margarine
1 cup thin green bell pepper strips
1 (15-ounce) can pineapple chunks, drained
$1/2$ cup barbecue sauce

Preheat gas grill using medium setting. Toss the rice and butter lightly in a bowl. Add the green pepper strips, pineapple and barbecue sauce and mix well. Divide the rice mixture evenly among six 8x12-inch pieces of heavy-duty foil. Double fold the foil at the top; fold the edges securely. Place the packets directly on the grill. Grill for 10 to 15 minutes per side, turning once.

   Yield: 6 servings

BAKED APPLES

2 apples, cored, cut into quarters
2 teaspoons brown sugar
$1/8$ teaspoon cinnamon, or to taste
$1/8$ teaspoon nutmeg, or to taste
1 teaspoon lemon juice
$1/4$ cup water

Preheat oven to 450 degrees. Place the apples in a baking pan. Sprinkle with a mixture of the brown sugar, cinnamon and nutmeg. Pour a mixture of the lemon juice and water around the apples. Bake for 25 minutes or until the apples are tender.

   Yield: 2 to 3 servings

GINGERED CRANBERRY SAUCE

1 pound fresh cranberries, rinsed, sorted
1/2 cup sugar, or to taste
3 strips lemon zest
2 cinnamon sticks
1 (1/2-inch) piece fresh gingerroot, thinly sliced
1/4 cup apple cider or Jack Daniel's whiskey
1/4 cup ginger brandy or orange juice

Combine the cranberries, sugar, lemon zest, cinnamon sticks, gingerroot, apple cider and ginger brandy in a large saucepan. Bring to a boil; reduce the heat. Simmer for 10 minutes or until of the desired consistency. Cool completely. Remove and discard the lemon zest, cinnamon stick and gingerroot. Cover the cranberry sauce and chill for 1 hour or longer before serving. Keeps for up to 3 weeks in the refrigerator. For extra flavor, leave the lemon zest, cinnamon and gingerroot in the sauce until just before serving.

Yield: 8 to 12 servings

NEVER-FAIL HOLLANDAISE SAUCE

1/2 cup frozen butter
1 1/2 tablespoons lemon juice
3 egg yolks

Combine the butter, lemon juice and egg yolks in a double boiler over hot water. Cook until thickened, stirring constantly with a wooden spoon or whisk and making sure to scrape the mixture away from the side and bottom of the pan.

Yield: 8 servings

DESSERTS

DESSERTS

AMARETTO CAKE

1 cup sliced almonds
1 (2-layer) package yellow cake mix
1 (4-ounce) package vanilla instant pudding mix
4 eggs
1/2 cup amaretto
1/2 cup vegetable oil
1/2 cup cold water
Amaretto Glaze

Preheat oven to 350 degrees. Sprinkle the almonds in a greased and floured 12-cup tube pan or bundt pan. Combine the cake mix, pudding mix, eggs, amaretto, oil and cold water in a bowl and mix well. Spoon into the prepared pan. Bake for 1 hour. Cool in the pan for 10 minutes. Invert onto a serving plate. Pierce the cake several times with a skewer. Drizzle Amaretto Glaze over the cake.

Yield: 16 servings

AMARETTO GLAZE

1/2 cup butter
1 cup sugar
1/2 cup amaretto

Combine the butter, sugar and amaretto in a saucepan. Cook over medium heat for 5 minutes or until of glaze consistency, stirring constantly.

MAMA'S BANANA NUT CAKE

2 cups self-rising flour
2 cups sugar
4 eggs
1 cup vegetable oil
4 bananas, mashed
2 cups pecan pieces

Preheat oven to 350 degrees. Mix the flour, sugar, eggs, oil, bananas and pecans in a bowl. Spoon into a greased bundt pan. Bake for 1 hour or until the cake tests done.
  Yield: 16 servings

CHRISTMAS NUT CAKE

1 pound dates, chopped
1 pound candied cherries, chopped
1 pound pecans, chopped
$1/2$ cup self-rising flour
$1^1/2$ cups margarine or butter, softened
$2^1/2$ cups sugar
6 eggs
3 tablespoons vanilla extract
3 cups self-rising flour

Dredge the dates, candied cherries and pecans with $1/2$ cup flour. Set aside. Cream the margarine and sugar in a mixer bowl until light and fluffy. Beat in the eggs 1 at a time. Beat in the vanilla. Add the flour 1 cup at a time, beating well after each addition. Stir in the dates, candied cherries and pecans. Spoon into a greased tube pan. Bake at 250 degrees for 2 hours or until the cake tests done. May be baked in 2 greased loaf pans for 1 hour. Best if baked at Thanksgiving and allowed to age until Christmas.
  Yield: 25 to 35 servings

CREAM CARAMEL CAKE

$2^2/_3$ cups flour
$1/_4$ teaspoon baking soda
1 teaspoon salt
1 cup butter, softened
3 cups sugar
6 eggs
1 cup sour cream
1 tablespoon vanilla extract
Caramel Frosting

Preheat oven to 350 degrees. Sift the flour, baking soda and salt together. Cream the butter and sugar in a mixer bowl until light and fluffy. Beat in the eggs 1 at a time. Add the flour mixture and sour cream alternately, beating well after each addition. Stir in the vanilla. Spoon into 3 greased and floured 9-inch cake pans. Bake for 25 to 35 minutes or until the layers test done. Cool in the pans for 10 minutes. Remove to a wire rack to cool completely. Spread Caramel Frosting between the layers and over the top and side of the cake.

Yield: 12 servings

CARAMEL FROSTING

4 cups confectioners' sugar
1 cup butter
2 cups packed light brown sugar
$1/_2$ cup evaporated milk
$1/_2$ teaspoon vanilla extract

Place the confectioners' sugar in a large bowl. Melt the butter in a saucepan. Add the brown sugar and evaporated milk. Cook over medium heat for 2 minutes, stirring constantly. Remove from the heat. Stir in the vanilla. Pour over the confectioners' sugar. Beat until smooth and of spreading consistency.

RED VELVET CAKE

1 to 2 ounces red food coloring
2 tablespoons baking cocoa
1/2 cup shortening
1 1/2 cups sugar
2 eggs
2 1/4 cups flour
1 teaspoon (scant) salt
1 cup buttermilk
1 teaspoon vanilla extract
1 teaspoon baking soda
1 tablespoon vinegar

Preheat oven to 350 degrees. Make a paste of the food coloring and cocoa in a small bowl and set aside. Cream the shortening, sugar and eggs in a mixer bowl until light and fluffy. Add the cocoa paste. Add the flour, salt, buttermilk and vanilla. Add the baking soda and vinegar alternately, beating just until mixed. Spoon into 2 greased and floured 8-inch cake pans. Bake for 30 minutes. Cool in the pans for several minutes. Remove to a wire rack to cool completely. Spread a favorite cream cheese frosting between the layers and over the top and side of the cake.

Yield: 12 servings

GRILLED CAKE WITH LEMON CREAM

1 (10-ounce) angel food cake or pound cake, cut into 3/4-inch slices
3/4 cup lemon pie filling
1/4 cup sour cream
1 tablespoon lemon juice
whipped topping

Preheat gas grill using medium setting. Grill the cake slices for 2 to 3 minutes per side or just until lightly browned. Blend the pie filling, sour cream and lemon juice in a bowl. Spoon over the cake slices. Top with whipped topping.

Yield: 10 servings

PLUM CAKE WITH CONFECTIONERS' SUGAR GLAZE

2 cups self-rising flour
2 cups sugar
1 cup vegetable oil
3 eggs, beaten
1 teaspoon ground cloves
1 teaspoon cinnamon
2 (4-ounce) jars baby food plums
Confectioners' Sugar Glaze

Preheat oven to 325 degrees. Combine the flour, sugar, oil, eggs, cloves, cinnamon and plums in a bowl and mix well. Spoon into a greased bundt pan. Bake for 1 hour or until the cake tests done. Cool in the pan for several minutes. Invert onto a serving plate. Drizzle with Confectioners' Sugar Glaze. Editor's Note: See page 156 for the nutritional profile of this recipe.

Yield: 15 servings

CONFECTIONERS' SUGAR GLAZE

1/3 cup chopped walnuts or pecans
1/2 cup confectioners' sugar
juice of 1/2 lemon

Combine the walnuts and confectioners' sugar in a bowl and mix well. Add the lemon juice gradually, stirring constantly until of glaze consistency.

UGLY DUCKLING CAKE

1 (2-layer) package yellow cake mix
1 (16-ounce) can fruit cocktail
1 cup flaked coconut
2 eggs
1/2 cup packed brown sugar
1/2 cup chopped pecans or walnuts
1/2 cup butter
1/2 cup sugar
1/2 cup evaporated milk
1 1/3 cups flaked coconut

Preheat oven to 325 degrees. Combine the cake mix, undrained fruit cocktail, 1 cup coconut and eggs in a mixer bowl. Beat at medium speed for 2 minutes. Spoon into a greased 9x13-inch cake pan. Sprinkle with the brown sugar and pecans. Bake for 45 minutes. Boil the butter, sugar and evaporated milk in a saucepan for 1 minute. Stir in 1 1/3 cups coconut. Spoon the mixture over the warm cake. May top with whipped topping.

Yield: 15 servings

TOASTED SWEET TREATS

1/2 cup margarine or butter, melted
2 teaspoons grated orange peel
8 (3/4-inch) slices pound cake
2 cups orange sections
3/4 cup chocolate sauce
2 cups whipped cream

Preheat gas grill using medium setting. Mix the margarine and orange peel in a small bowl. Brush over both sides of the cake slices. Place the cake slices on the grill. Grill for 3 to 5 minutes per side or until golden brown. Arrange the cake slices on a serving plate. Top with the orange sections, chocolate sauce and whipped cream.

Yield: 8 servings

COUNTRY APPLE TART

$1/2$ (15-ounce) package frozen all ready pie crusts, thawed
4 medium apples, peeled, cut into $1/2$-inch slices
1 to 2 tablespoons sugar
$1/4$ teaspoon ground cinnamon
$1/16$ teaspoon ground nutmeg
2 tablespoons margarine or butter, cut into pieces

Preheat gas oven to 425 degrees. Place the thawed crust on an ungreased baking sheet. Arrange the apples in a circular pattern over the crust, leaving a $1\frac{1}{2}$-inch border. Sprinkle with a mixture of the sugar, cinnamon and nutmeg. Dot with the margarine. Fold the edge of the crust over the apples. Bake for 15 minutes or until the apples are tender and the crust is golden brown.
   Yield: 8 servings

CREAM CHEESE PIE

1 cup sugar
13 ounces cream cheese, softened
6 ounces whipped topping
$1/4$ cup toasted pecans
1 (9-inch) graham cracker pie shell

Cream the sugar and cream cheese in a mixer bowl until light and fluffy. Stir in the whipped topping and pecans. Spread in the pie shell. Chill until serving time.
   Yield: 8 servings

PECAN PIE

$1/2$ cup butter or margarine
1 cup sugar
4 eggs
1 cup dark corn syrup
1 cup pecan pieces
1 teaspoon vanilla extract
1 unbaked (9-inch) pie shell

Preheat oven to 350 degrees. Brown the butter in a skillet. Pour into a bowl. Add the sugar and mix well. Beat in the eggs 1 at a time. Add the corn syrup and mix well. Stir in the pecans and vanilla. Spoon into the pie shell. Bake for 30 to 45 minutes or until a knife inserted near the center comes out clean.
  Yield: 8 servings

PEPPERMINT PIE

6 tablespoons margarine, softened
1 bar German's sweet chocolate
3 cups cocoa-flavored crisp rice cereal
$1/2$ gallon peppermint ice cream, slightly softened

Mix the margarine, sweet chocolate and cereal in a bowl. Press into a pie plate. Spread the ice cream over the chocolate mixture. May serve with hot fudge sauce. Pie will keep no longer than 2 to 3 days.
  Yield: 8 servings

DESSERTS

SWEET POTATO PIE

2 pounds sweet potatoes, peeled, chopped

3/4 cup sugar

3 egg yolks

1 cup melted margarine

1 teaspoon nutmeg

1 teaspoon each vanilla extract and lemon extract

1 cup evaporated milk or half-and-half

3 egg whites, stiffly beaten

1 unbaked (9-inch) pie shell

Preheat oven to 350 degrees. Cook the sweet potatoes in water to cover in a saucepan until tender; drain well. Mash the sweet potatoes in a bowl. Add the sugar, egg yolks, margarine, nutmeg, vanilla extract and lemon extract and beat well. Add the evaporated milk. Fold in the egg whites. Spoon into the pie shell. Bake for 1 1/2 hours.

Yield: 8 servings

WHITE APPLE BROWNIES

2/3 cup butter, softened

1 cup packed brown sugar

1 cup sugar

2 eggs

1 teaspoon vanilla extract

2 cups sifted flour

1/2 teaspoon salt

1/2 cup each chopped pecans and chopped peeled apple

3/4 cup confectioners' sugar

Preheat oven to 350 degrees. Cream the butter, brown sugar, sugar, eggs and vanilla in a mixer bowl until light and fluffy. Add the flour and salt and mix well. Fold in the pecans and apple. Spoon into a greased 8x12-inch baking pan. Bake for 40 minutes. Cool in the pan before cutting into bars. Dust with confectioners' sugar. Editor's Note: See page 156 for the nutritional profile of this recipe.

Yield: 36 servings

CHESS SQUARES

1 (2-layer) package butter-recipe yellow cake mix
1 egg
1/2 cup margarine, softened
3/4 cup chopped pecans (optional)
3 ounces cream cheese, softened
2 eggs
1 (16-ounce) package confectioners' sugar

Preheat oven to 350 degrees. Combine the cake mix, 1 egg, margarine and pecans in a bowl; mix well with a fork. Press into a 9x12-inch baking pan. Beat the cream cheese in a mixer bowl until light and fluffy. Beat in 2 eggs. Add the confectioners' sugar gradually, beating constantly. Spoon over the cake mix mixture. Bake for 40 to 45 minutes or until golden brown. Let cool before cutting into squares.
   Yield: 18 to 24 servings

CHOCOLATE CHIP SQUARES

6 tablespoons melted margarine
1/2 cup packed brown sugar
1/2 cup sugar
1 egg
1 teaspoon vanilla extract
1 cup self-rising flour
3/4 cup miniature semisweet chocolate chips
3/4 cup pecan pieces

Preheat oven to 350 degrees. Combine the margarine, brown sugar, sugar and egg in a bowl and beat well. Blend in the vanilla and flour. Fold in the chocolate chips and pecans. Spread in a greased and floured 8x8-inch baking pan. Bake for 30 to 35 minutes or until set. Let cool before cutting into squares.
   Yield: 16 servings

DESSERTS

CHOCOLATE KISS SURPRISES

1³/4 cups sifted flour
1 teaspoon baking soda
¹/2 teaspoon salt
¹/2 cup butter, softened
¹/2 cup peanut butter
¹/2 cup sugar
¹/2 cup packed brown sugar
1 egg
1 teaspoon vanilla extract
¹/4 cup sugar
1 (16-ounce) package milk chocolate kisses

Preheat oven to 375 degrees. Sift the flour, baking soda and salt together in a bowl. Beat the butter and peanut butter in a mixer bowl until smooth.

Add the sugar and brown sugar to the peanut butter mixture and beat until fluffy. Add the egg and vanilla and mix well. Add the flour mixture gradually, beating well after each addition.

Shape the mixture into balls. Roll in ¹/4 cup sugar. Place on nonstick cookie sheets. Bake for 8 minutes. Remove from the oven. Press a candy kiss onto each cookie. Bake for 2 to 3 minutes longer or until browned.

Yield: 7 dozen

DESSERTS

RAISIN HONEY DROPS

2 cups sifted flour
1 teaspoon each (heaping) salt and cinnamon
$1/2$ teaspoon (heaping) baking soda
$3/4$ cup each honey and sugar
$3/4$ cup butter or margarine, softened
1 egg
2 cups rolled oats
1 cup raisins

Preheat oven to 375 degrees. Sift the flour, salt, cinnamon and baking soda together and set aside. Cream the honey, sugar, butter and egg in a mixer bowl until light and fluffy. Add the flour mixture and mix well. Stir in the oats and raisins. Drop by heaping teaspoonfuls onto a greased cookie sheet. Bake for 12 to 14 minutes or until lightly browned. Cool on a wire rack.

Yield: 4 dozen

GINGERBREAD MEN

$2 1/4$ cups flour
$1/2$ cup sugar
$1/4$ cup butter, softened
$1/2$ cup molasses
1 egg
$1 1/2$ teaspoons ground cinnamon
1 teaspoon ground ginger
$1/4$ teaspoon ground cloves
small raisins

Combine the flour, sugar, butter, molasses, egg, cinnamon, ginger and cloves in a large mixer bowl. Beat at medium speed until mixed. Chill, covered, for 1 hour. Preheat oven to 350 degrees. Roll the chilled dough $1/8$ inch thick on a lightly floured surface. Cut out with a gingerbread man cutter. Place $1/2$ inch apart. on a cookie sheet. Decorate with raisins for eyes, nose, mouth and buttons. Bake for 8 minutes or until browned. May be decorated with frosting when cool.

Yield: $1 1/2$ to 2 dozen

FRENCH QUARTER STRAWBERRY CHEESECAKE

1 (10-ounce) package frozen strawberries, thawed
1 cup sour cream
$^1/_4$ cup sugar
16 graham crackers, crushed
$^1/_4$ cup butter, softened
24 ounces cream cheese, softened
4 egg yolks
$^3/_4$ cup sugar
1 teaspoon vanilla extract
4 egg whites, stiffly beaten
2 cups sour cream
$^1/_4$ cup sugar

Combine the strawberries, 1 cup sour cream and $^1/_4$ cup sugar in a bowl and mix well. Chill, tightly covered, until needed.

Preheat oven to 350 degrees. Lightly oil the bottom of a 9x13-inch baking dish. Combine the graham cracker crumbs and butter in a bowl and mix well. Press over the bottom of the prepared baking dish.

Combine the cream cheese, egg yolks, $^3/_4$ cup sugar and vanilla in a large mixer bowl. Beat until creamy and smooth. Fold in the egg whites. Spoon the batter carefully over the graham cracker mixture. Bake for 40 minutes or until lightly browned. Remove from the oven.

Combine 2 cups sour cream and $^1/_4$ cup sugar in a bowl and mix gently. Spoon carefully over the baked layer. Bake for 5 minutes. Let stand until cool.

Spoon the strawberry mixture over the cheesecake. Chill until serving time.

Yield: 15 to 18 servings

BANANAS FOSTER CHEESECAKE

3 cups graham cracker crumbs
3/4 cup melted butter
36 ounces cream cheese, softened
1 cup sour cream
4 eggs
1 cup sugar
1 tablespoon vanilla extract
1 tablespoon banana liqueur

Preheat oven to 350 degrees. Combine the graham cracker crumbs and melted butter in a bowl and mix well. Press onto the bottom and up the side of a 10-inch springform pan. Chill until the crust has hardened somewhat.

Combine the cream cheese and sour cream in a mixer bowl. Beat until blended and smooth. Fold the eggs, sugar, vanilla extract and banana liqueur into the cream cheese mixture. Spoon over the crust in the springform pan.

Place the springform pan in a larger pan partway filled with water. Bake for 2 hours or until a wooden pick inserted near the center comes out clean. Cool in the pan. Remove the side of the pan. Cut the cheesecake into slices.

Yield: 14 servings

HOLIDAY CHOCOLATE CHIP CHEESECAKE

8 ounces cream cheese, softened
1/2 cup sugar
1 egg
1 cup chocolate chips
1 1/2 cups flour
1/4 cup baking cocoa
1/2 teaspoon salt
1/2 cup vegetable oil
1 cup sugar
1 teaspoon vanilla extract
1 teaspoon baking soda
1 cup water
1 tablespoon vinegar

Preheat oven to 350 degrees. For the topping, beat the cream cheese, 1/2 cup sugar and egg in a mixer bowl until blended. Stir in the chocolate chips and set aside.

For the batter, blend the flour, cocoa, salt, oil, 1 cup sugar, vanilla, baking soda, water and vinegar in a bowl; the batter will be thin. Spoon into a greased 8x8-inch baking pan. Spoon the topping over the batter and swirl through with a knife.

Bake for 50 to 60 minutes or until a wooden pick inserted near the center comes out clean. Let cool before cutting into squares.

Yield: 16 servings

STRAWBERRY FROZEN DESSERT

1 cup sifted flour
$1/4$ cup packed light brown sugar
$1/2$ cup chopped walnuts
$1/2$ cup melted butter or margarine
2 egg whites
1 cup sugar
2 cups sliced fresh strawberries
2 tablespoons lemon juice
1 cup whipping cream, whipped

Preheat oven to 350 degrees. Mix the flour, brown sugar, walnuts and butter in a bowl until crumbly. Spread evenly on a 12x18-inch baking sheet. Bake for 20 minutes or until browned, stirring occasionally. Sprinkle $2/3$ of the crumb mixture in a 9x13-inch baking pan, reserving the remainder for a topping.

Combine the egg whites, sugar, strawberries and lemon juice in a large mixer bowl. Beat for 10 minutes or until stiff peaks form. Fold in the whipped cream. Spoon the strawberry mixture over the crumb mixture in the baking pan. Top with the reserved crumb mixture. Freeze for 8 hours. Cut into squares and garnish with whole strawberries.

May substitute one 10-ounce package frozen strawberries, partially thawed, for the fresh strawberries and reduce the sugar to $2/3$ cup. Editor's Note: See page 156 for the nutritional profile of this recipe.

Yield: 12 servings

♨ BANANAS AND BROWN SUGAR

4 bananas, unpeeled, cut lengthwise into halves
1/2 cup sour cream or sour half-and-half
1/4 cup packed dark brown sugar
1/4 cup toasted slivered almonds

Preheat gas grill using medium setting. Place bananas peel side down on the grill. Grill for 5 to 10 minutes or until the peels are black. Turn the bananas. Grill for 2 to 3 minutes longer. Place the bananas on serving plates. Top with the sour cream, brown sugar and almonds. Editor's Note: See page 156 for the nutritional profile of this recipe.

Yield: 4 servings

MICROWAVE PEANUT BRITTLE

1$\frac{1}{2}$ cups shelled raw peanuts
1 cup sugar
1/2 cup light corn syrup
1/8 teaspoon salt
1 teaspoon margarine
1 teaspoon vanilla extract
1 teaspoon baking soda

Mix the peanuts, sugar, corn syrup and salt in a 1$\frac{1}{2}$-quart microwave-safe glass container. Microwave on High for 8 minutes, stirring once. Stir in the margarine. Microwave for 2 minutes. Stir in the vanilla. Add the baking soda, stirring quickly until light and foamy. Pour onto a lightly greased baking sheet or into a lightly greased glass casserole, spreading as thinly as possible. Let cool and break into pieces. Store in an airtight container.

Yield: 1 pound

🔥 BUNUELOS

8 (6-inch) flour tortillas
1/4 cup vegetable oil
1/4 cup melted margarine or butter
1/2 cup sugar
1/2 teaspoon cinnamon
2 pints vanilla ice cream
1/2 cup clover honey

Preheat gas grill using medium setting. Brush both sides of each tortilla with a mixture of the oil and margarine. Grill the tortillas for 4 to 5 minutes per side or until golden brown. Sprinkle with a mixture of the sugar and cinnamon. Top with the ice cream; drizzle with the honey.

Yield: 8 servings

🔥 FRUIT HASH

1/2 cup packed dark brown sugar
1/4 cup flour
1/4 teaspoon nutmeg
1/2 cup cold margarine or butter, cut into pieces
2 cups pineapple chunks
1 cup raspberries
1 cup blueberries
1/2 cup chopped toasted pecans
2 pints vanilla ice cream

Preheat gas grill using medium setting. Combine the brown sugar, flour and nutmeg in a medium bowl. Cut in the margarine until crumbly. Place the pineapple, raspberries and blueberries in an 8x8-inch baking pan. Sprinkle with the brown sugar mixture and pecans. Grill, covered with heavy-duty foil, for 20 to 30 minutes or until bubbly. Serve over scoops of ice cream. Editor's Note: See page 156 for the nutritional profile of this recipe.

Yield: 8 servings

GIRDLE BUSTER

1/2 cup butter

2 cups confectioners' sugar

6 tablespoons baking cocoa

1/2 (12-ounce) can evaporated milk

1 (16-ounce) package Oreo cookies, crushed

1/2 cup melted butter

vanilla ice cream, softened

16 ounces whipped topping

chopped pecans or walnuts (optional)

maraschino cherries (optional)

Melt 1/2 cup butter in a medium saucepan. Add the confectioners' sugar and cocoa, stirring until blended. Add the evaporated milk gradually, stirring until the confectioners' sugar dissolves. Bring to a boil; remove from the heat. Set aside to cool completely. Press a mixture of the cookie crumbs and 1/2 cup melted butter into a lasagna pan or 9x13-inch glass dish. Spread with the ice cream. Spoon the cocoa mixture over the top. Freeze until firm. Top with whipped topping, pecans and cherries.

Yield: 12 to 15 servings

MORE AND MORE S'MORES

24 graham crackers

1 1/2 cups marshmallow fluff

12 milk chocolate peanut butter cups

Preheat gas grill using medium setting. Spread the graham crackers with marshmallow fluff. Place half the graham crackers marshmallow side up in a 9x13-inch baking pan. Top each with 1 peanut butter cup and 1 graham cracker. Grill, covered with heavy-duty foil, for 3 to 5 minutes or until the chocolate is melted.

Yield: 12 servings

DESSERTS

SOUTHERN DELIGHT

1½ packages Pepperidge Farm Bordeaux cookies, crushed
¼ cup melted margarine
1 quart pralines and cream ice cream, softened
1 package almond brickle chips
1 quart vanilla ice cream, softened
1 jar caramel ice cream topping
toasted pecans

Mix the cookie crumbs and margarine in a bowl. Press into a freezer-proof pan. Freeze until firm. Spread with the pralines and cream ice cream. Sprinkle with most of the almond brickle chips. Spread with the vanilla ice cream and top with the caramel topping. Sprinkle with the remaining almond brickle chips and pecans. Freeze until serving time. Keeps 1 week in the freezer.

Yield: 12 to 15 servings

🔥 TROPICAL SUNDAES

6 (½- to ¾-inch) pineapple slices
½ cup sparkling white wine or ginger ale
½ teaspoon finely chopped crystallized ginger
1 pint lemon sorbet or lemon sherbet
½ cup toasted flaked coconut

Arrange the pineapple slices in a shallow glass baking dish. Add the wine and ginger. Marinate for 30 minutes. Preheat gas grill using medium setting. Remove the pineapple from the marinade, reserving the remaining marinade. Grill the pineapple for 5 minutes per side. Serve in shallow bowls with the reserved marinade. Top with scoops of lemon sorbet and sprinkle with coconut. Editor's Note: See page 156 for the nutritional profile of this recipe.

Yield: 6 servings

NUTRITIONAL PROFILE GUIDELINES

We have attempted to present these family recipes in a format that allows approximate nutritional values to be computed. Persons with dietary or health problems or whose diets require close monitoring should not rely solely on the nutritional information provided. They should consult their physicians or a registered dietitian for specific information.

NUTRITIONAL PROFILE ABBREVIATIONS

Cal — Calories	T Fat — Total Fat	Sod — Sodium
Prot — Protein	Chol — Cholesterol	g — grams
Carbo — Carbohydrates	Fiber — Fiber	mg — milligrams

Nutritional information is computed from information derived from many sources, including materials supplied by the United States Department of Agriculture, computer databanks and journals in which the information is assumed to be in the public domain. However, many specialty items, new products and processed foods may not be available from these sources or may vary from the average values used in these profiles. More information on new and/or specific products may be obtained by reading the nutrient labels. Unless specified, the nutritional profile of these recipes is based on all measurements being level.

✦ **Artificial sweeteners** vary in use and strength so should be used "to taste," using the recipe ingredients as a guideline. Sweeteners using aspartame (NutraSweet and Equal) should not be used as a sweetener in recipes involving prolonged heating, which reduces the sweet taste. For further information on the use of these sweeteners, refer to the package.

✦ **Alcoholic ingredients** have been analyzed for the basic ingredients, although cooking causes the evaporation of alcohol, thus decreasing caloric content.

✦ **Buttermilk**, **sour cream**, and **yogurt** are commercial types.

✦ **Cake mixes** that are prepared using package directions include 3 eggs and 1/2 cup oil.

✦ **Chicken**, cooked for boning and chopping, has been roasted.

✦ **Cottage cheese** is cream-style with 4.2% creaming mixture. Dry curd cottage cheese has no creaming mixture.

✦ **Eggs** are all large. To avoid raw eggs that may carry salmonella, as in eggnog or 6-week muffin batter, use an equivalent amount of commercial egg substitute.

✦ **Flour** is unsifted all-purpose flour.

✦ **Garnishes**, serving suggestions, optional information, and variations are not included.

✦ **Margarine** and **butter** are regular, not whipped or presoftened.

✦ **Milk** is whole milk, 3.5% butterfat. Low-fat milk is 1% butterfat. Evaporated milk is whole milk with 60% of the water removed.

✦ **Oil** is any type of vegetable cooking oil. **Shortening** is hydrogenated vegetable shortening.

✦ **Salt** and other ingredients to taste as noted in the ingredients are not included in the profile.

✦ If a choice of ingredients is given, the profile reflects the first option. If a choice of amounts is given, the profile reflects the greater amount.

Pg. No.	Recipe Title (Approx Per Serving)	Cal	Prot (g)	Carbo (g)	T Fat (g)	% Cal from Fat	Chol (mg)	Fiber (g)	Sod (mg)
35	Seafood Pasta Chowder	345	13	34	17	45	60	1	596
36	Brunswick Stew	262	21	37	4	14	32	10	337
36	Gary's Chicken Soup	337	31	32	10	27	133	3	247
41	Cream of Spinach Soup	158	11	16	5	31	10	3	695
45	Mother's Cranberry Salad Ring	217	2	46	4	16	0	2	28
46	Simple Pasta Salad	333	5	27	23	61	20	2	176
48	Salmon Caesar Salad	533	48	7	33	58	143	1	350
50	Fruit and Yogurt Coffee Cake	244	4	37	10	34	44	2	224
64	Roquefort Flank Steak	218	26	1	12	50	67	<1	249
68	Beef Roast with Jalapeño Corn Bread Stuffing[1]	308	42	10	10	30	134	2	243
70	Chuck Wagon Roast[2]	281	35	6	11	37	105	<1	197
71	Cajun Pork Chops[5]	285	20	1	22	70	75	<1	379
72	Szechuan-Style Spareribs[2]	895	63	6	66	68	259	1	539
73	Dijon Ham and Swiss	800	42	107	22	25	132	5	1171
74	Microwave Ham and Potatoes	314	20	30	13	37	73	2	531
75	Grilled Ham[2]	355	36	18	14	37	70	<1	1829
79	Honey Pineapple Chicken Breasts[2]	336	27	52	3	8	73	<1	76
79	Peppercorn Chicken	172	18	2	4	23	55	<1	113
81	Chicken Tandoori[2]	283	35	7	12	39	105	<1	438
82	Orange-Scented Chicken[3]	255	36	4	10	35	108	1	108
83	Apricot Ginger Chicken[2]	399	36	27	16	37	108	<1	124
83	Orange-Glazed Cornish Hens[2, 4]	476	56	40	9	18	233	2	282
84	Grilled Turkey with Italian-Style Rice Stuffing[1]	564	73	23	18	29	184	1	864
85	Braised Turkey Shanks	246	22	8	14	53	59	1	793
92	Orange Roughy in Layers[3]	117	23	2	1	10	31	1	102
94	Lemon Snapper[2]	314	31	1	20	58	56	<1	68
95	Whole Red Snapper San Francisco[3]	279	37	17	6	21	61	2	360
98	Seared Sesame-Glazed Ahi Tuna Steaks[2]	697	57	36	36	47	105	<1	898
99	Fish Fillets with Capers and Dill	126	25	1	2	12	71	<1	216
99	Sea Scallop Kabobs with Melon	178	9	5	14	70	18	<1	314
100	Crab Cakes	395	18	15	29	66	121	1	690
101	Rémoulade Sauce	543	<1	2	59	98	53	<1	745
105	Shrimp and Chicken Sauté[6]	382	34	11	22	50	186	3	416

NUTRITIONAL PROFILES

Pg. No.	Recipe Title (Approx Per Serving)	Cal	Prot (g)	Carbo (g)	T Fat (g)	% Cal from Fat	Chol (mg)	Fiber (g)	Sod (mg)
105	Shrimp Cypress Inn	666	38	21	48	64	274	1	1139
107	Light Fettuccini Alfredo	354	18	50	9	23	15	6	365
108	Hot Pasta Primavera	243	10	31	10	37	7	4	300
109	Easy Spinach Lasagna	410	26	41	17	36	95	6	1169
110	Tri-Color Veggie Pasta	303	12	32	15	43	41	3	191
111	Vegetable and Cheese Pie	289	18	9	21	64	161	2	363
112	Eggs in a Ring	363	14	36	18	45	128	4	885
116	Green Beans Mediterranean	78	2	9	5	50	0	3	123
118	Baked Carrots	100	1	11	6	51	16	3	389
124	Oven French Fries	84	2	15	2	24	0	1	5
127	Grill-Baked Sweet Potatoes with Apricot Butter[7]	218	2	36	9	34	23	4	135
138	Plum Cake with Confectioners' Sugar Glaze[8]	349	3	47	17	44	43	1	226
142	White Apple Brownies	124	1	19	5	35	21	<1	73
149	Strawberry Frozen Dessert	297	3	32	18	54	48	1	98
150	Bananas and Brown Sugar	262	3	44	10	33	13	4	23
151	Fruit Hash	386	4	43	24	54	29	3	193
153	Tropical Sundaes[2]	166	1	34	2	10	0	1	35

[1]Nutritional profile includes entire amount of stuffing.

[2]Nutritional profile includes entire amount of marinade and/or basting mixture.

[3]Nutritional profile does not include vegetable oil.

[4]Nutritional profile does not include margarine.

[5]Nutritional profile includes entire amount of dry rub.

[6]Nutritional profile does not include butter for sautéing almonds.

[7]Nutritional profile includes entire amount of apricot butter.

[8]Nutritional profile includes entire amount of glaze.

INDEX

INDEX

INDEX

ORDER INFORMATION

<table>
<tr><td rowspan="5">MAIL ORDERS TO:
Seacoast Publishing, Inc.
P.O. Box 26492
Birmingham, AL 35260</td><td></td><td>Qty.</td><td>Total</td></tr>
<tr><td>SIMPLY SOUTHERN $18.95 per book</td><td></td><td></td></tr>
<tr><td>Alabama residents add $1.50 per book sales tax</td><td></td><td></td></tr>
<tr><td>Shipping $2.50 per book</td><td></td><td></td></tr>
<tr><td>Total enclosed</td><td></td><td></td></tr>
</table>

Name:

Address:

City: State: Zip:

Make checks payable to Seacoast Publishing, Inc.

<table>
<tr><td rowspan="5">MAIL ORDERS TO:
Seacoast Publishing, Inc.
P.O. Box 26492
Birmingham, AL 35260</td><td></td><td>Qty.</td><td>Total</td></tr>
<tr><td>SIMPLY SOUTHERN $18.95 per book</td><td></td><td></td></tr>
<tr><td>Alabama residents add $1.50 per book sales tax</td><td></td><td></td></tr>
<tr><td>Shipping $2.50 per book</td><td></td><td></td></tr>
<tr><td>Total enclosed</td><td></td><td></td></tr>
</table>

Name:

Address:

City: State: Zip:

Make checks payable to Seacoast Publishing, Inc.

This page may be photocopied.